United Methodist Women Purpose

The organized unit of United Methodist Women shall be a community of women whose purpose is to know God and to experience freedom as whole persons through Jesus Christ; to develop a creative, supportive fellowship; and to expand concepts of mission through participation in the global ministries of the church.

The Vision

Turning faith, hope and love into action on behalf of women, children and youth around the world.

Living the Vision

We provide opportunities and resources to grow spiritually, become more deeply rooted in Christ and put faith into action.

We are organized for growth, with flexible structures leading to effective witness and action.

We equip women and girls around the world to be leaders in communities, agencies, workplaces, governments and churches.

We work for justice through compassionate service and advocacy to change unfair policies and systems.

We provide educational experiences that lead to personal change in order to transform the world.

 # Table of Contents

🔔 Introduction

On the day of the feast of unleavened bread, Jesus gathered with his disciples. They drank, ate, and shared stories. It seemed like a normal Passover meal, but at one point Jesus did something unexpected. He took bread, lifted it up, blessed it, broke it, and gave it to each disciple saying: "Take, eat: this is my body." As they sat there, probably perplexed and wondering what Jesus meant, he took a cup of wine, blessed it, and asked each disciple to drink from the cup; for this was his "blood of the covenant"(Matthew 26:26–28; Mark 14:22–24).[1]

With those simple words, God through Jesus continued the act of divine covenant making with the people of God, this time with Jesus' disciples. Every instance in the First Testament when God made a covenant it changed the lives of people, and this was no exception. Our God is in the covenant-making business, yet, most of us have not studied this foundational way in which God intercedes for us and interacts with us. We are inclined to speak of the Old and New Testaments, which can lead us to invalidate the commandments of the First Testament. In doing this, we may devalue our Jewish sisters and brothers because, in effect, we are saying that if the old covenants and the Old Testament have been replaced, then they are a people of no covenant and no testament. For this reason, I shall refer to the First Testament (instead of the Old Testament) and the Second Testament (instead of the New Testament) in this book. The divine covenants throughout the Bible lie at the core of our faith and delineate our relationship with God. James L. Garlow writes that divine covenant is foundational to "our understanding of salvation, holiness, healing, worship, deliverance, and sanctification."[2]

Covenants are found in the Bible from the moment God created man and woman until the last page of Revelation. Several types of covenants are found in the Bible. There are divine covenants that are between God and human beings, and covenants between individuals and nations. Recall that in decades past all that was needed was a handshake to seal an agreement. Or, you may remember as a child becoming "blood brothers or sisters" when you and your best friend pricked a finger and rubbed them together. These common actions are rooted in the process of covenant making that we find in ancient Israel and some other cultures of long ago.

When I was about five years old, my best friend Arty and I took a safety pin, opened it up, poked our fingers and held them together and told each other that we would be friends forever. During the years that we lived on the same block, Arty came to my rescue many times.

He stepped in front of a bully, helped me get up when I fell, and looked out for my well-being. I, in turn, was there for him when he got in trouble at home or school, and about once a week Mom and I baked some cookies for Arty and me to share. We were bound together by this tiny act. There was something inherently sacred about this simple childhood action of making a blood bond. Even though we did not have the words for it, we knew it was something that should not be broken.

It was not until I was in my thirties that I discovered that the bond Arty and I made was a covenant, and that something similar happened in the Bible. I learned about it in the early 1980s at a Wednesday night Bible study, where we read the story about Jonathan and David. They made a covenant with each other that was sealed by blood. There were severe consequences for not honoring this bond:

> To Jonathan and David this (covenant) was a serious commitment that the sons of Israel did not take lightly. A way of life that ordered your steps and altered your lifestyle, from your relationships with others to the way you conducted your affairs, all under the watchful eye of an omnipresent God.[3]

As the Wednesday night group continued to study the significance of the bond between Jonathan and David, I began to look at God in a whole new light. Until that moment, God had been some uninterested force that created the universe and had no time to care for me. Now, though, I read and heard that it was because of David and Jonathan's knowledge of the divine covenants God had made, and because they understood that God would never revoke a covenant, that they could trust each other to uphold their covenantal agreement. I saw that God cared about each of them and the sanctity of their individual relationship with God, and thus with each other. What occurred between them happened under God and with God. It was a sacred bond, a holy bond.

It was a revelation that opened my heart. I saw the Bible with new eyes and noticed that God cares enough about human beings and the earth to enter into a sacred relationship and establish a divine covenant, not just once but time and time again. Our ancestors of faith knew this and they understood the importance and sacredness of covenants. As noted by Norbert Lohfink, biblical scholar, "In the period of the second temple, even before the appearance of Jesus, 'covenant' was almost a standard word among Jewish people for their ancestral religion."[4] Covenant was core to their understanding of God's interactions with humanity throughout the centuries. Even when they turned their backs, God did not abandon them. God had made covenantal promises that were unable to be revoked.

You and I make a promise for a day and sometimes cannot keep it. We enter into a contract and then may hunt for a way to make it null and void. Even our marriage vows are subject to cancellation. Human contracts or promises may be created out of unjust and selfish motives. Sometimes there can be a blessing in ending a harmful contract. Yet, alone we cannot make covenantal promises that will last for a lifetime or beyond. Only God is capable of that.

Covenants do not only apply to individuals such as Arty and myself or biblical figures such as David and Jonathan. They are not limited to those that you or I may make with God; they are also integral to living in a faith community.

This becomes clearly evident with the Covenant of Guidance and Law that God made with Moses for all the Israelites. We see it, again, as Jesus brings the disciples together and in the early community of Christ followers that is found in Acts. As we explore these covenants, we will discover that covenantal living calls us to acts of mercy and justice, not only with those in our community, but with all, regardless of their social, political, financial, or religious standing. Through covenantal living, we are connected to God, others, and the whole creation.

In the United Methodist tradition (in which I am an ordained elder) there is a rich history of covenantal living. John Wesley, an Anglican priest and founder of Methodism, knew that people needed guidance to live faithfully in community.

Wesley began his own search in 1725 when the direction of his life changed and he wanted to discover how to express his faith in practical ways. Wesley's exploration of deeper faith "led him to tie together the perfectionism of the pietists, the moralism of the Puritans, and the devotionalism of the mystics."[5] These realizations took root when Wesley went to Oxford and formed a club later called "Methodists." This newly formed group "not only devoted itself to prayer and Bible study, they also reached out to some persons in jail and to others with various special needs."[6]

It was apparent to John Wesley that faith needed to be lived out with others who came together as a committed group that held one another accountable for how they spent their time and for their actions in the world. Though this was not defined as a covenantal relationship, it had the markings of one.

John Wesley wrote guidelines for a covenant service in 1780 as a way of encouraging Christians to renew their covenant with God. In Wesley's mind, our covenant with God should be made not only in our hearts, but also in our words. He directed the community of the faithful to write down the covenant in their own words as "a memorial of the solemn transactions that have passed between God and [believers]."[7] Different versions of Wesley's Covenant

Service are still commonly held today on New Year's Eve or Day. Wesley's own covenant prayer is a powerful model of ritualizing our covenantal relationship with God. A key point in the covenant service occurs when worshippers say in one voice this prayer that ends with the recognition of God's covenant "made on earth" and to be "ratified in heaven."[8]

As we grow to understand the divine covenants made by God with our ancestors, and thus with us, our faith and our lives will transform. Our responses to God's covenants, like Wesley's prayer, will guide our lives towards greater compassion and openness. This study will enhance your understanding of how God works with us, in us, and through us. The biblical witnesses powerfully show us that covenants are God's gifts to humanity through which we may truly live as those who bear the image of God.[9]

The Covenants

We will begin with the first divine covenant in the Bible: God's promises to Adam and Eve, and also look at God's call for a new covenant through the prophet Jeremiah. Between those two were four major divine covenants that God made with the Israelites as they became a nation. We will learn how God formed this tribe and the implications for us today. Finally, we will explore the everlasting and eternal covenant that we have with God through Christ Jesus. The covenants are not named in the Bible. These terms were coined by me to make the covenants easy to remember and to distinguish them from each other.

In our study we will look at:

1. The Covenant of Care and Grace, which is the first divine covenant between God and the earliest humans in the Bible, Adam and Eve, found in Genesis 1:27–30 and Genesis 3:20–21.

2. The Covenant of Redemption and Safety, which came after the flood. This covenant was between God, Noah, and all future generations. This story is found in Genesis 6–9.

3. The Covenant of Blessing, which was between God and Abraham. Here the promise of a great nation was given. The foundational scripture is Genesis 15.

4. The Covenant of Guidance and Law, which was given to Moses on Mount Sinai. These were laws to live by as the Israelites put their days of pilgrimage in the desert behind them upon entering the Promised Land, and are laws for both then and now. This study focuses on three sections of scripture related to this important covenant: Leviticus 25, Deuteronomy 9–11, and Exodus 19–20.

5. The Covenant of Eternal Rule, which is God's divine covenant with David. Related to this is the covenant between David and Jonathan (1 Samuel 18:1–4). God's covenant with David is found in 2 Samuel 7 and 1 Chronicles 17. In addition we will look at Jeremiah 31.

6. The Everlasting Covenant: The Covenant of Redemption and Grace, which is the covenant we have through Jesus and encompasses all of God's previous covenants. It is the foundation for anyone professing to be a Christian. The foundational texts for this covenant are: Luke 22:7–23 and Matthew 26:17–30.

Each covenant reveals a new dimension of humanity's relationship with God and with each other. The covenants do not stand alone, but instead build on each other. The latter covenants do not supersede the earlier ones. When the people failed to keep a covenant, there was not an alternative divine plan that God could have called "Plan B." God did not scrap the human model for something else. God continued and continues to work through us to make God's will evident on earth as it is in heaven. Our covenant agreement with God can be summarized as learning to love God with all of our heart, all of our soul, all of our mind, and all of our strength. Through this study, my prayer is that we come to marvel at our covenant God, grow in our love for God, for each other, and for our neighbors near and far.

One image that is important to me for understanding the interrelatedness of all the divine covenants is water. Water in the Bible is a sign of both creative and destructive power. Water as a symbol of divine grace points to renewal, cleansing, and new life. Creation began in the waters of chaos. Life began again after the waters of the flood. The sea was parted so the Israelites could survive. Water came from a rock when they were thirsty in the desert. In Isaiah, we hear God's invitation for all who are thirsty to come to the water (Isaiah 55:1). Jesus entered the waters of baptism at the onset of his ministry. In his conversation with the Samaritan woman at the well, Jesus assured that those who drink of him would never be thirsty again (John 4:14). Water also indicates life-threatening forces. The flood brought forth death. The same water that was parted to give safe passage to the Israelites engulfed the lives of the Egyptians that pursued them. In these cases, we are challenged to find God's grace in spite of the deadly presence of water.

As you begin this study, I invite you to place an empty pitcher on the table in front of you. With each of the divine covenants add some water and watch the pitcher get fuller and fuller. As the Israelites continued to be in a covenantal relationship with God, they grew from a wandering people to a nation. When we reach the Everlasting Covenant we discover that with Jesus our pitcher over-flows, symbolizing the waters of our baptismal covenant that connects us.

My prayer is that you will see how each covenant encompasses the other, coming to a fullness and completion in Jesus' life, death, and resurrection. In order for us to take this journey together, I need to say a word about how I read scripture. First of all, I look for what type of writing it is: poetry, story, history, parable, song, or a wisdom saying. Next, I study about the time and place it was written. This helps me understand its context. Finally, I look at what precedes and follows the text. None of this diminishes the message because all of the stories in the Bible are sacred stories; each with its own meaning.

We will start with an exploration into what a covenant is and is not; the traditional form of covenant making and how God calls us to live in a covenantal community. Through this journey may you discover new ways to engage your community and become agents of transformation through a commitment to enter fully into partnership with God's Everlasting Covenant.

Endnotes

1. The story of the last meal Jesus shared with his disciples is recorded in all Gospels and Paul's First Letter to the Corinthians. The United Methodist Great Thanksgiving liturgy follows 1 Corinthians 11:23–26 most closely.

2. James L. Garlow, *The Covenant: A Study of God's Extraordinary Love for You* (Kansas City: Beacon Hill Press, 2007), 13.

3. Kay Arthur, *Our Covenant God: Living in the Security of His Unfailing Love* (Colorado Springs, CO: Waterbrook Press, 1999), 83.

4. Norbert Lohfink, translated by John J. Scullion, S. J., *The Covenant Never Revoked: Biblical Reflections on Christian-Jewish Dialogue* (New York: Paulist Press, 1991), 7.

5. Richard P. Heitzenrater, *Wesley and the People Called Methodists* (Nashville: Abingdon Press, 1995), 31.

6. Donald B. Strobe, *United Methodism: The Accidental Church* (Madison Heights, MI: Cathedral Directories, 1990), 3.

7. John Wesley, "Wesley's Covenant Service, Directions for Renewing Our Covenant with God 1780," in Frank Whaling, ed., *John and Charles Wesley Selected Writings and Hymns* (Mahwah, NJ: Paulist Press, 1981), 145.

8. Ibid., 147. For the entire text of Wesley's Covenant Prayer, please see the epilogue of this book or *The United Methodist Hymnal* (1989), #607.

9. Dr. Michael Fitch and Geoff Hawley write, "From Genesis to Revelation, we see that God does not condescend to mankind's level but rather enables mankind (who are God's image bearers) to approach His level through His covenants," in *Covenants, Creation and Choice: Where Theology and Science Overlap* (Bloomington, IN: WestBow Press, 2013), 4.

 CHAPTER 1

Overview of Covenants

From the beginning, God extended grace to human beings. This grace "is the common thread that seems to unite the divine covenants of the Old Testament," and our self-revealing God "chooses a people for relationship, not out of obligation or need but purely due to sovereign choice."[1] The first divine covenant that we read about in the Bible occurred between God and the first named human being, Adam, though the word "covenant" is never used. In order to understand divine covenants and what God intended for us, we need to know what a covenant is and is not.

Introduction to Covenants

Throughout most of my young adult life I saw no difference between the words "promise," "contract," and "covenant." In my mind each one of these were subject to the whims of one of the two parties and could be negated with minimal, if any, consequences. So, I looked at Merriam-Webster's dictionary for the definitions of these words.*

Promise: a statement telling someone that you will definitely do something or that something will definitely happen in the future.

Contract: a legal agreement between people or companies that is negotiable.

Covenant: a formal and serious agreement between people or companies.[2]

---

*By permission. From Merriam-Webster's Collegiate® Dictionary, 11th Edition, ©2016 by Merriam-Webster, Inc. (www.Merriam-Webster.com).

I discovered that the English word for covenant is derived from the Latin *con venir*, which means to come together.

These three definitions lead us to see what biblical covenants are. They are not a prediction or a statement of what will happen in the future; they are not a legal binding agreement that could be resolved through the courts or arbitration; it is not just between people or companies. While we find many covenants in the Bible such as the one between David and Jonathan, a divine covenant is initiated by God and made with an individual who may be the representative for an entire nation or all believers.

> Divine covenants come in two varieties, unilateral and bilateral. With a unilateral covenant, God imposes the covenant terms and conditions associated with it. With a bilateral covenant there is commitment from both sides. A timescale is given for when the covenant is in force. A bilateral covenant has one additional ingredient when compared to a unilateral covenant: ratification that involves the sprinkling or shedding of blood. A token or a sign is often given by God, and a celebration meal is usually held.[3]

Covenantal agreements have been found to exist in antiquity. In the ancient cultures, even prior to the formation of Israel, covenant making between kings or between a king and a vassal was common. Historians trace the making of covenants as far back as the Hittites who "lived and ruled before the covenant was inaugurated at Mount Sinai."[4] Their treaties or covenants were used to exercise control over those who had been conquered while giving them room to self-govern within the framework of the signed covenant. These covenants followed a particular pattern, which was fairly well replicated in the covenants of the First Testament.

Some of the early Israelite leaders, such as Moses, would have been familiar with these Hittite covenants. Moses would have understood that these were binding agreements that had consequences both for keeping and breaking them.[5] From the beginning, God used a style of covenantal language that would be familiar to God's people; a style without the need for instructions or definitions of terms. We have a covenant-making God who keeps the covenant, reveals God's self through the covenant, and enables us to fulfill our part of the covenant. When we went astray in the past, God stood by us because of the divine covenants; this continues to be true today.

Biblical Definition of Covenant

FIRST TESTAMENT

As I grew up, I never heard the word "covenant" used, nor did I understand its importance in my relationship with God. Over the centuries, we have lost the richness of its meaning. Most of us no longer clearly recognize how God worked with covenants as God's people went from a tribal existence to a kingdom and then a nation.

There are over 250 instances in the First Testament where the Hebrew word for "covenant" (*berîth*) is used.[6] From the beginning, God desired to be in relationship with us.

Most often we see in the First Testament the phrase for "to make a covenant" (*kārat berîth*).[7] These words are central to understanding our covenant God and the process by which God makes covenants with us. While there is debate among scholars as to the exact origin of *kārat berîth*, as we look at the definitions of these Biblical covenants, we will begin to uncover their richness.

Berîth is the key word for "covenant." When it is used between nations it is a treaty, which leads to alliances for each other's protection. Between individuals it is a pledge or agreement to do something or not do something. Divine covenants, those between God and humans, are accompanied by signs, sacrifices, and a solemn oath seals the relationship with promises of blessing for keeping the covenant and curses for breaking it.[8]

This definition tells us that when we enter into a covenant—especially with God, but also with one another—it is a sacred joining. It is considered to be a bond of life and death. As we shall see, Jesus brought the divine covenant that God initiated with Adam full circle. All of the divine covenants, including the one Jesus represents, were established solely by the prerogative of God.[9]

Kārat, another key Hebrew word when studying covenants, is a verb that means "to cut off, cut down, fell, cut or make."[10] The Israelites understood the phrase *kārat berîth* to literally mean to cut a covenant. This indicated that God initiated the covenant. This was a solemn oath or promise sealed in blood. When it occurred between individuals such as David and Jonathan, they would slit their wrists, hold their arms together, and mingle their blood; the two became one.

Two parties could also cut an animal in two as a way of sealing a covenant. This was usually a bull, a goat, or a lamb. Rob Board, pastor, theologian, and author of *The Power of God's Blood Covenant with You*, brings a new and different perspective when he describes covenant making in the following manner. Once the animal was split in two, the two individuals would stand back-to -back between the two halves and walk around each half in a figure eight and face each other when they returned to the center. In an online article Board goes on to say that the figure eight represented the length of time the covenant was in effect—for infinity. This signified a never-ending relationship.[11]

While speculative, this understanding does highlight the importance of a relationship that endures. We shall see that when God made the divine covenant with Abraham, it was only God who moved between the two halves of the bull ram. In addition to sealing the covenant with blood, a pledge was often spoken where each person affirmed that if the covenant was broken, it would be done to the person who failed to uphold the covenant as it was done to the animal whose blood was shed. This was serious business, and shows us how important all the covenants are.

Not all of the covenants found in the Bible were sealed in blood, but all of them represented a sacred vow, a holy communion between the parties.

When God made a covenant, God declared the intention to remain in relationship with us for eternity. Therefore, whenever any one of us feels hopeless, worthless, or lost, we are to remember that God chose to cut a divine covenant with us and send grace and forgiveness into our lives.

This applies not only to us as individuals, but also to our faith communities. There are times when we fail to act as God calls us. We may remain silent instead of speaking out against injustice; hold hate or prejudice toward certain people and fail to act with compassion. Even then, God does not write us off because we are in a covenantal relationship. This does not mean that we can ever justify human sins and wrongs. It is in the midst of our human inabilities and failures that God continues to call us to partner with God in moving our communities to greater justice and compassion.

SECOND TESTAMENT

In the Second Testament, we discover the Greek word for "covenant" (*diatheke*). It has a somewhat different meaning than *berîth* and carries a more legalistic tone. Remember that Greek society was highly structured, with courts of law and rules for its citizens. It is interesting to note that *diatheke* is not the legal word for "covenant," but perhaps it was the term used in everyday language.

According to W. E. Vine, "Diatheke primarily signifies a disposition of property by a will. In its use in the Septuagint it is the rendering of a Hebrew word meaning covenant or agreement."[12] The word implies an arrangement made between two parties, where one party can accept or reject it but may not alter it.[13] The only way the conditions of a covenant can be changed is to make a new one; not even God would change an existing divine covenant. This is stated clearly in Galatians 3:15 where it is written: "Brothers and sisters, I give an example from daily life: once a person's will has been ratified, no one adds to it or annuls it."

What Is the Purpose of a Covenant?

FROM OUR HUMAN VIEWPOINT

As we study the major covenants, it will become clear that God called us from the time of Adam for the purpose of being in a relationship where we would care for the earth, each other, and ourselves. When God made the divine covenant with Israel, those tribes became bound to God. God in turn protected and provided for them. Time and again we hear of God's acts of mercy and kindness proclaimed by the Psalmists with awe and wonder. To enter into a covenant with God does not mean that we will never have problems, trials, or losses in life. We can be confident, however, that God will lead us through life's joys and pains. God will never abandon us, nor will God arbitrarily change the conditions of God's agreement with us. This gives us the assurance that God wants to remain in relationship and will continue to guide us, through Jesus and the Holy Spirit, if we will listen.

FROM GOD'S PERSPECTIVE

God's covenants are a tool by which we can measure our faithfulness to the Holy One, or our lack of it. Through the voices of the prophets in the First Testament we hear them call the Israelites back into their covenant relationship whenever they have strayed. One such prophet, Hosea "observed how Israel had rejected God and broken the covenant. He said, 'You were my people, but now you are not my people' (Hosea 1:9)."[14] Hosea was issuing a strong reminder to those around him that they did not want to abandon God's plan for them and go off on their own. God simply wants us to be committed and dedicated enough to follow God instead of the ways of the world. God calls us into communion where we can experience all the mercy, grace, forgiveness, and restoration that we need. Through all of the divine covenants, and particularly the everlasting covenant which Jesus established, God has provided a means by which we can always be reconciled to God and live in the manner that we are called to by God.

WHAT IT MEANS

Stop for a moment and think about Abraham, Sarah, Moses, Miriam, David, and Paul, as well as the Israelites and the early Christian communities. Each individual and community was singled out by God for a great purpose and each acknowledged their relationship with the Almighty. Yet, they failed at some point. Abraham and Sarah did not initially believe that God would give them a child in their older years. Moses killed a man and ran. Miriam did not follow God's instructions. David was a king chosen by God for leadership at a critical time, yet his lust for a woman led him to adultery and murder. Paul admitted that he saw through a glass darkly, and at times did what he knew he should not do and did not do what he knew he should. Despite how each individual turned away from God, or how the community may have failed to act, God did not cast them aside or go looking for those who would be more faithful.

For many years, I believed I was not good enough for the church. At that time I was living in Seattle, Washington, and involved in several social justices movements. I thought that my life was fine yet something was missing. No matter how much I did, I never felt worthy or saw that my work made a difference.

In those days, I often went to the university bookstore coffee shop to read or write. Across the street from it was a United Methodist church. One day, when I turned down that street, I read a sign out in front of the church that said, "Early Christians. Breakfast at 8:00 a.m. Service at 8:30 a.m. All are welcome." I "heard" a gentle whisper in my mind that said, "Try it out."

Now, I had taken a stand against organized religion many years before and there was no way I would walk into a church. Yet each time I drove down that street, I heard those words again. What did I do finally? I stopped driving down that street. I did not want to face the possibility of being rejected again because of my disability and my sense that God had forgotten me.

All of that changed on a quintessential sunny afternoon when Seattle sparkled like its nickname, "The Emerald City." I turned down that street without thinking, and I heard that voice again only now it seemed to yell in my mind, "TRY IT OUT!" "All right," I responded. "I will go once and then, God, leave me alone!"

The next Sunday, filled with an uncertainty bordering on fear, I walked into that church. Almost immediately, I started to turn and walk out again when I was greeted by a woman named Jean. She touched my shoulder, smiled, and welcomed me. The warmth and sincerity of her expression sent a wave of relaxation that cascaded down me like a waterfall. I smiled back and settled into a seat next to her and her husband. At the end of the service Jean introduced me to several people. As I talked with and listened to her friends a feeling began to rise within me that I had not experienced for decades; it was the sense of coming home. This was not what I was expecting. I was confused but their genuine, kind words were enough to keep me coming back. Though, for many months I remained unsure that God loved me because there had been far too many years when I had felt defective and thrown away by God.

Jean kept inviting me back, and I kept accepting the invitation. One day, she asked me to go to the Wednesday night Bible study. The only reason I even tried it out was because Jean asked me to and I wanted to get to know her better. My very first evening there we began to talk about our covenant-making God. I was intrigued and returned nearly every Wednesday. During those weeks, I heard stories of people in the Bible who had done horrific deeds, who felt abandoned by God and yet God did not turn away. One night when Jean and I were talking, I began to realize that God had a divine covenant with me that God would never break. I was the one who had turned away and blamed God for everything that was wrong with my life.

There was not an immediate reconciliation. My realizations, though, placed me on a journey that slowly nudged me closer to accepting God's love. Over time I began to see myself as one of God's beautiful creations. In the words of a common saying, "God does not make junk," therefore none of us are defective. As I began to accept the truth that God had initiated a divine covenant with me and everyone else, I was able to embrace the truth that God's love for me was unfailing—no matter what I had done. Through the weeks that I attended this Bible study, I became aware that if more and more of us who say we are disciples knew this truth in our hearts we would begin to see new ways to live with each other in a covenantal community.

The Call to Be a Covenantal Community

As we shall discover, from the beginning God's care for us was unconditional and all we had to do was follow God's call to care for all that was created. We were to be in union with each other, with God, and with God's work that was called "good." In making a covenant with us there is only one thing that God expected from us: commitment. Commitment to live as people made in the image of the Holy One. Commitment to keep our word. Commitment to remember and act on God's overarching love for each one of us.

We find the powerful affirmation of humanity made in the image of God in Genesis: "Let us make humankind in our image, according to our likeness" (Genesis 1:26a). The plurality of "us" in this passage does not necessarily mean multiple gods. Rather it points more to the communal nature of God, a recognition of the inner community within God. *Imago Dei*—creation in the image of God—is a significant theological idea indicating that humanity is made to be in community. Created in the likeness of God, human beings are to resemble the communal and Trinitarian life of God.

In the development of the theology of Trinity in the early church, this communal nature of God was further defined to be an egalitarian and harmonious relationship. *Perichoresis*, the Greek term that in general means to move around, was used by early church theologians to explain the dynamic inner life of God. Theologian Karen Baker-Fletcher translates *perichoresis* as "dance" and writes, "We are the miracle when we live in the wholeness of divine grace toward all creation . . . This is the dance with God!"[15] Elizabeth Johnson, another theologian, similarly writes that our triune God "dynamically moves around the others, interacts with the others, interweaves with the others in a circling of divine life."[16] The divine persons in the Trinity dance together to bring new life to humans and all creation.

The orthodox faith emerged as early Christian struggled to clarify who God was in light of the life, death, and resurrection of Jesus and the coming of the Holy Spirit. The theology of the Trinity shed light on how the Creator, Jesus Christ, and the Holy Spirit all work together to bring salvation for all. There were theologies that attempted to establish hierarchy among the Trinity. The process of coming together in the Trinitarian theology in the early church was not easy. By the time the Nicene-Constantinople Creed was adopted in the fourth century, however, the church was able to agree that each person in the triune God was equally divine, equally powerful, and equally important and that all were part of one living God.

The divine *perichoresis* gives us a vision for the ideal human community. We are called to be nonhierarchical, egalitarian, and compassionate toward one another, as the three persons in the Trinity are. This is the vision of community the prophets proclaimed and Jesus embodied. The Trinity gives us a powerful vision of life, and as Jung Young Lee puts it, "Life is none other than Trinitarian."[17] In the Trinitarian community, the gap between poor and rich is resisted, harming others in any way is condemned and considered unethical, and all are invited to the abundant and transforming life in God.

Covenant was at the heart of Israel's religion.[18] It brought the people into community and created a way for them to relate to each other. Through guidance from God and their leaders they learned to work together, care for those who could not care for themselves, and develop festivals that were practical signs of "their gratitude for life, their repentance for having violated their covenant commitment, or their need for God's assistance."[19]

The rhythm of Israel's covenantal community centered on the weekly sabbath. This was a time for rest and reflection, not just for themselves but for everyone, even those who worked for them, most of whom were not Israelites. Eventually, the idea of the weekly sabbath was expanded to the proclamation of the Jubilee, the year of the Lord's favor. As instructed in Deuteronomy 15, the Israelites were instructed to free slaves, both male and female, and forgive debts every seventh year. The year of the Jubilee expressed care and concern for the disadvantaged and guided human communities to live out God's call for justice. In his first public teaching as recorded in Luke, Jesus quoted Isaiah on this very topic of the Jubilee:

> The Spirit of the Lord is upon me,
> because he has anointed me
> to bring good news to the poor.
> He has sent me to proclaim release to the captives
> and recovery of sight to the blind,
> to let the oppressed go free,
> to proclaim the year of the Lord's favor.
> (Luke 4:18–19)

In this speech, Jesus made his mission and call clear: to bring forth a community of radical love. Yet, people were so enraged to hear the message that they drove him out of the town and attempted to kill him (Luke 4:28–29). Jesus' death on the cross did not happen as an accident at the end of his ministry, but was implicated from the beginning of his first teaching. Jesus called for a covenantal community in which wealth was shared, the poor were fed, and the marginalized were given power. This was the vision of the Trinitarian community. Crucifixion was a consequence of people's rejection of such a vision. As Easter people, Christians are called to embody Jesus' vision everyday.

Methodism, as John Wesley structured it, was a blueprint for a Christian covenantal community and a practical way to live out Jesus' teachings. He knew that weekly preaching was not enough to form committed Christians who would make a difference in the world. In his experience recurrent practices combined with participation in acts of mercy were critical components for Methodists to live in a covenantal relationship with each other and with God.

In addition to the ordinances of God which were: regular attendance in worship, study of scripture, fasting, communion as often as possible, and prayer, Wesley created general rules that all who called themselves Methodist were to follow. We were to be divided into classes with twelve people in each class plus a leader. This class would covenant to do no harm, doing good as far as possible to everyone (not just Methodists or other Christians), and hold each other responsible to live according to those ordinances.[20]

Covenant is a call to community and it requires a commitment from each one of us to learn more about the requirements that God has set in each of the major covenants and God's call on our lives. God created us to live in covenant with all that is holy; in covenant with our neighbors and in covenant with ourselves. As we learn how to do this, we will transform ourselves, our communities, and even the world. Churches today are challenged to be a model of God's covenantal community and called to work to bring forth healing and reconciliation in the midst of pain and suffering.

THE THREE ASPECTS OF GOD IN A COVENANT

In understanding covenants, there are three aspects of God to consider: God the covenant maker, God the covenant keeper, and God the covenant equipper. These are not three independent actions of God. Rather they are interrelated and essential to the holistic picture of our covenantal God.

God the covenant maker: In our divine covenants, God is the initiator. As the covenant maker, God establishes a relationship with us and commits to be in that relationship for eternity. From the beginning of our history as a tribal people through today, our leaders attempt to make treaties and covenants that will bind us in peace, and protect us from our enemies. Yet, we fail time and time again. Without God in the mix, we will forever be unable to live in harmony with others. However, if we choose to accept God's invitation to covenantal living and covenantal community, the way is laid out for us to be able to care for our earth and its inhabitants.

God the covenant keeper: God is not just the covenant maker; God is also the covenant keeper. The truth that people turned from God again and again is not limited to what we read in the Bible; we do it all the time. We break our sabbath, we destroy animals and plants and peoples created by God to the point of extinction, we shout hate rhetoric at people we do not understand or like—we turn our backs again and again. Yet, we can be forever grateful that God does not turn away from us. God actively oversees and administers the covenants. These covenants are divine and eternal, but we also have to choose to come to God on God's terms or to walk away. It does not matter if we agree with them or not. God is in charge, and God is attempting to make it clearly evident that we are cared for and will not be left alone to survive on our own devices if we choose rightly.

Divine covenants are "sovereignly administered . . . No such thing as bargaining, bartering, or contracting characterizes the divine covenants of Scripture."[21] This may be difficult to accept in these days of everything being relative; where truth is based on our interpretation of it and becomes truth only when we accept it. This clearly would leave God out of the covenant-making business. The truths of these divine covenants have informed lives for thousands of years. As we grow to understand how they apply to our lives today, they will continue to inform our actions and our deeds. When we commit to covenantal living, God is right there to show us the way through Jesus. Christ embodies the previous covenants (which we shall see later). By God's grace, we are given the keys to living as a kingdom of people in a divine relationship with the triune God.

God the covenant equipper: God is the covenant equipper. Perhaps you have heard the phrase: "God does not call the equipped; God equips the called." Even when Adam and Eve failed miserably, God provided them with the means to continue in the redefined relationship with God. They were so ashamed and did not know what to do, but God knew and showed them; though now there was a different set of rules. We cannot know what it will ultimately look like to commit to our covenant relationship with God, but when we say yes to God's covenant with us, our lives will be formed by a new set of guidelines. Perhaps each of us will find a new view of life, and a confidence in our abilities that we never dreamed possible—a confidence that is not rooted in our egos or our accomplishments but in our covenant God.

Redefining Old Covenant and New Covenant

Before we embark upon the study of the divine covenants, it is important to rid ourselves of thinking of the old covenants, those found in the First Testament, as less important than the new covenant found in the Second Testament as initiated by Christ Jesus. We may have a tendency to believe that the covenants of the First Testament are not applicable to our lives as Christians. Remember that Jesus said: "Do not think that I have come to abolish the law or the prophets; I have come not to abolish but to fulfill" (Matthew 5:17). This is a statement about all that God had done throughout our history as the people of God, and provides a glimpse into what God expects of us where we are today.

Speaking of the "Old" and "New" Testaments does not always lead us to invalidate the commandments of the First Testament. Doing this, however, may cause us to devalue our Jewish sisters and brothers. There is a danger in saying that the old covenants and the Old Testament have been replaced, because the implication is that Jews are a people of no covenant and no testament. This thinking contributes to anti-Semitism. It can lead to an unconscious belief that there are two gods: the God of the Old Testament and the Christian God. Nothing could be further from the truth. As we embrace both testaments and all the covenants, our lives will be immensely enriched, and we will be able to build better relationships with our Jewish neighbors. Studying God's covenants is one way to reclaim our Judeo-Christian heritage.

The concept of an old covenant or covenants is found only once in the Second Testament and that is in 2 Corinthians 3:14. I always find it interesting how we can read something in only one place and have it take on such a divisive significance. Yet in that verse "no opposition between the two 'covenants' is set up there, nor is there an end to the 'old' when the 'new' comes."[22]

Jesus did not introduce the idea of a new covenant. It is mentioned for the first time in Jeremiah 31:31–34. There the prophet speaks of a covenant that will be written on the hearts of those who believe in the one true God:

> The days are surely coming, says the Lord, when I will make a new covenant with the house of Israel and the house of Judah. It will not be like the covenant that I made with their ancestors when I took them by the hand to bring them out of the land of Egypt—a covenant that they broke, though I was their husband, says the Lord. But this is the covenant that I will make with the house of Israel after those days, says the Lord: I will put my law within them, and I will write it on their hearts; and I will be their God, and they shall be my people. No longer shall they teach one another, or say to each other, "Know the Lord," for they shall all know me, from the least of them to the greatest, says the Lord; for I will forgive their iniquity, and remember their sin no more.

This was not just a future prediction about Christ Jesus bringing a new/ everlasting covenant because all the prophets spoke also to the people of their day. They spoke of possible calamities and potential blessings. The Israelites had not kept their covenantal agreement with God. Yet, God's grace still surrounded them; they were still God's people. God came to them again through the prophet Jeremiah with a new divine covenant. This covenant would be given to them in another way. Now, it would be something from within each person, the Torah would be written on everyone's heart.

This covenant embraced the earlier ones, and through God the Israelites were given the way to return to living as God had directed them. In a sense, God pardoned them, remembered their sins no more and instituted a new beginning. What God was promising was that if the people would accept God's terms, there would be an end to exile and a return to their home.

As we study the covenants found in the Bible, we will discover that from the beginning God has formed us, shown us the way to live, and given us a path to sustain life on earth and to live together with all of God's people.

Endnotes

1. Chris Woodall, *Covenant: The Basis of God's Self-Disclosure* (Eugene, OR: Wipf & Stock, 2011), xii.

2. *Merriam-Webster's Collegiate Dictionary*, 11th ed., (Springfield, MA: Merriam-Webster, 2003), s.v. "promise," "contract," "covenant."

3. Dr. Michael Finch and Geoff Hawley, *Covenants, Creation and Choice: Where Theology and Science Overlap* (Bloomington, IN: WestBow Press, 2013), xvii.

4. J. Maurice Wright, *God's Covenant Plan: Living in Him* (Maitland, FL: Xulon Press, 2011), 33.

5. Ibid., 36.

6. Jack W. Hayford, executive editor, *People of the Covenant* (Nashville, TN: Thomas Nelson, 2011), 2.

7. Jared T. Parker, "Cutting Covenants," Religious Studies Center, accessed September 26, 2016, https://rsc.byu.edu/archived/gospel-jesus-christ-old-testament/7-cutting-covenants.

8. Elmer Smick, "Covenant," *Theological Workbook of the Old Testament,* vol. 1, ed. R. Laird Harris, Gleason L. Archer, and Bruce Waltke (Chicago: Moody Press, 1980), 128.

9. Woodall, *Covenant: The Basis of God's Self-Disclosure*, xi.

10. Kay Arthur, *Our Covenant God: Living in the Security of His Unfailing Love* (Colorado Springs, CO: WaterBrook Press, 1999), 32.

11. "The Blood Covenant—Why Is It Important to Understand?" The Covenant Kingdom, accessed August 24, 2015, www.the-covenant-kingdom.com/blood-covenant-steps.html.

12. W. E. Vine, *Expository Dictionary of New Testament Words* (London: Oliphants, Ltd., 1948), 250.

13. Guy Duty, *God's Covenants and Our Time* (Minneapolis: Bethany Fellowship, Inc, 1964), 7.

14. Wright, *God's Covenant Plan: Living in Him*, 22.

15. Karen Baker-Fletcher, *Dancing with God: The Trinity from a Womanist Perspective* (St. Louis, MO: Chalice Press, 2006), 169.

16. Elizabeth Johnson, *Quest for the Living God* (New York: Bloomsbury Academic, 2007), 127.

17. Jung Young Lee, *The Trinity in Asian Perspective* (Nashville, TN: Abingdon Press, 1997), 180.

18. Dianne Bergant, CSA, *People of the Covenant: An Invitation to the Old Testament* (Franklin, WI: Sheed & Ward, 2001), 14.

19. Ibid., 15.

20. *The Book of Discipline of The United Methodist Church,* "The Nature, Design, and General Rules of Our United Societies," ¶104 (Nashville: Abingdon Press, 2012), 76.

21. O. Palmer Robertson, *The Christ of the Covenants* (Phillipsburg, NJ: Presbyterian and Reformed Publishing, 1980), 15.

22. Norbert Lohfink, translated by John J. Scullion, S. J., *The Covenant Never Revoked: Biblical Reflections on Christian-Jewish Dialogue* (New York: Paulist Press, 1991), 35.

CHAPTER 2

The Covenant of Care and Grace and the Covenant of Redemption and Safety

The First Divine Covenant: The Covenant of Care and Grace

Even though the word "covenant" is not used until God's encounter with Noah, the first covenant we find is in Genesis 1 and 2. After creating the heavens and the earth, God said, "Let us make humankind in our image, according to our likeness; and let them have dominion over the fish of the sea, and over the birds of the air, and over the cattle, and over all the wild animals of the earth, and over every creeping thing that creeps upon the earth. So God created humankind in his image, in the image of God he created them; male and female he created them" (Genesis 1:26–27). Here is the God who trusted humankind with the care of creation. When God made us in the image of God, we were graciously brought in to a covenantal relationship with the creator.

While there are two creation stories, Genesis 1:1–2:4a and Genesis 2:4b–3:24, both traditions reflect the view of the world from Israel's ancient understandings. Let me first briefly describe the differences between these two creation accounts. The Genesis 1 creation story was written during the Jewish exile in Babylon in the sixth century BCE. Michelle A. Gonzales, assistant professor of the religious studies department at the University of Miami, aptly points out that "the trauma of the exile led Jews to write a creation narrative that emphasized God's power over chaos."[1] The creation of humankind is considered to be the culmination in God's cosmic creation. The creation narrative in Genesis 2 and 3 is from the oldest source of the Hebrew scripture dating back to the tenth century BCE. In this narrative, humanity is "at the front and center of creation."[2] These two stories belong to different literary genres as well: The Genesis 1 account is written more like poetry and serves as the preface to the Pentateuch (the first five books of the First Testament), while in contrast the Genesis 2 and 3 narrative offers a somewhat detailed personal characterization of the first human beings.

While I acknowledge such differences in these two creation stories, in this chapter I shall emphasize the commonalities between the two: Both narratives helped the ancient Israelites (and us today) understand their covenant relationship with God, the natural world that sustained them, and with each other. They both tell us that we were endowed with abilities and responsibilities based on God's covenant to care for us. Walter Brueggemann, one of the most thoughtful and studied theologians of the First Testament, states that, "It is best to use the word 'covenantal;' it affirms that the creator and the creation have to do with each other decisively. And neither can be understood apart from the other."[3] He tells us that this earliest covenant needs to be taken in a general sense as it is not as detailed or defined as later covenants.

UNDERSTANDING THE COVENANT

The first human beings, Adam and Eve, were in an intimate relationship with God and the "conditions of their continued fellowship were clearly spelled out in terms of benefits for obedience and penalties for unfaithfulness."[4] God loved all of creation and Adam and Eve were blessed by God and given the instructions to care for the plants and animals, to be fruitful and multiply. Every need was provided for and daily they walked with God, communed with God. From the beginning God made it known that God desired a personal relationship with human beings and that this relationship was pivotal to all others. There was a warning, though, that every tree of the garden was available for food, except one. Here came the cost of breaking this covenant: "The tree of the knowledge of good and evil you shall not eat, for in the day that you eat of it you shall die" (Genesis 2:17). However, God created man and woman with the ability to choose their actions; and the day came when the temptation to just taste the fruit of the tree of knowledge overcame their commitment to follow God's commands.

From theologian John C. L. Gibson's point of view the story of Adam and Eve is more symbolic than actual. Yet, this does not diminish what God revealed. As is noted in one Bible study resource, "Adam [and I would say Eve] is in each one of us, he is 'Everyman. That this world is not what it should be is due to man's disobedience of God."[5] The disobedience of Adam and Eve represents all the times each one of us chooses to act contrary to God's instructions for our lives. I agree that Genesis "chapter 3 describes not what happened in remote history . . . but the situation in which all human beings find themselves at the present time. . . . In the real life of human beings Paradise does not proceed disobedience but follows obedience."[6]

From the moment they ate the forbidden fruit both their and our covenant relationship with God was changed. From that time forward they could discern between good and evil; this was no longer left in God's domain. They, now, knew what was moral and what was not. Immortality was not to be in the domain of human beings, but the ability to choose moral behavior became their, and thus our, choice.

This first divine covenant "encompasses all successive covenants of redemption. It is a 'seed' covenant to the others which follow."[7] We should note that God moved swiftly in spite of their disobedience, and clothed Adam and Eve in coats of skin, instead of their self-made fig leaves. To do this, an innocent animal might have been sacrificed by God and, thus, even this first covenant was most likely bound by blood.

When we read about Adam and Eve and look at this story as the first covenantal relationship with God, we are introduced to the qualities found in the forthcoming covenants. In our attempt to understand how divine covenants are made we can see that:

1. God initiated the relationship.
2. God promised blessing.
3. God also promised judgment for breaking the covenant.
4. God used a blood sacrifice to seal the second part of the covenant after Adam and Eve broke the Covenant of Care.
5. God used the new skins for Adam and Eve to be the symbol of the seal of this covenant.

Understanding the Covenant's Relevance

WHAT DOES THE COVENANT SAY TO US TODAY?

When God instituted the Covenant of Grace, after Adam and Eve ate the fruit, God did not eliminate the Covenant of Care. From the moment human beings were created, God gave the directive for us to be appointed stewards over the earth. This has never changed. We have a call to be committed and obedient to God's command to maintain the splendor of creation, and God gave us the means by which to do this.

Each one of us, like Adam and Eve, has been called to honor our relational commitments towards God, each other, and all of creation. Through God's covenants, we are invited to be in community with one another. The idea of Ubuntu, thoughtfully explored by South African Archbishop Desmund Tutu, affirms that community is at the heart of our life.[8] Ubuntu, which roughly means, "I am because we are," comes from the Zulu/Xhosa expression "*ubuntu ungamntu ngabanye abantu* (each individual's humanity is ideally expressed in relationship with others.)"[9] Ubuntu challenges us to see that human beings are intimately connected with God and all other creations. It is in this symbiosis of all life that we cherish our covenantal relationship with God.

This divine covenant was initiated in trust and is still based on that. This trust is fundamental to all relationships, including our relationship with God.

God trusts us to do what we are called to do. Yet, even though God knows our weaknesses and that we will do what we know we should not do, God still established the Covenant of Grace and extended the Covenant of Care.

God is consistent even if we are not, and the love God felt for creation did not cease when Adam and Eve were disobedient. God came in grace to restore the fallen relationship. It is because of this initial covenant that we have the Everlasting Covenant with Christ Jesus and can be assured that every time we stumble, every time we turn our back on God, every time we sin, God's grace is there to lift us up and, as the psalmist said, "places our feet upon the rock making our steps secure" (Psalm 40:2).

HOW DOES THIS COVENANT INFORM OUR CHRISTIAN DISCIPLESHIP?

There have been many times in my life when I felt a nudge to turn left instead of right, to call someone, write a note, or be careful of the spilled water in the supermarket aisle. Too many times to count I had a rational reason to ignore that nudge, and more often than not there were negative consequences. I ran into a roadblock; a friend passed away; I slipped and fell. In nearly every instance, I recalled the nudge and once again pledged to follow those "God nudges." If I have them, I imagine that Adam and Eve had those same nudges and ignored them like I did. Even now, there are times when I do not follow through. The grace is that God keeps nudging not only me, but each one of us.

As a community of believers, we can begin to see that God's relationship with all of God's people is revealed initially in the Torah and begins with Adam and Eve. Theodore Hiebert, professor of the Old Testament, writes, "the Torah shows us that what we put in our mouths and consume with our minds will affect our well-being . . . and our relationship with others. . . . Covenant in the Bible is based on the relationships formed by the first human families."[10]

Our own Methodist heritage begins right with the creation story. John Wesley's first university sermon, which was preached at Oxford, was based on Genesis 1:27, "So God created humankind in his image." This statement is the basis of our understanding of Christian living. It "formed the foundation of Wesley's doctrine of the 'way of salvation.'"[11] Wesley tells us that when we see ourselves made as Adam and Eve were, in God's image, then we can know that this truth encompasses everyone and should lead us to realize that God's grace extends to the marginalized who have often been stripped of their dignity. Wesley frequently cautioned Methodists against being biased or bigoted. As United Methodists we need to live out this message through our church communities and be committed to actions that reflect our knowledge that all are made in the image of God.

The Covenant of Redemption and Safety

Gradually, the earth became filled with people who, over time, ignored the divine covenants God had established with Adam and Eve. They made up their own rules and lived according to their own design. Their lives revolved around what they wanted without concern for the earth or its inhabitants. Genesis 6:6 tells us that God was not angry but grieved and saddened that humankind had betrayed God's intention for all of creation. It was then that God made the decision to destroy all of creation, especially those human beings.

A possible scenario is that God, though, remembered how Adam and Eve had failed, but God had given them another chance to live out their covenantal relationship because God unconditionally loved them. So, God and the angels looked over the earth and found one man named Noah who had remained faithful to God. Walter Brueggemann reminds us, "God remembered Noah . . . His remembering is an act of gracious engagement with his covenant partner, an act of committed compassion. It asserts that God is not preoccupied with himself but with his covenant partner, creation."[12]

When God told Noah about the impending destruction of the world, Noah most likely was deeply troubled and confused, but he had faith. He believed God before it began to rain. He acted without fully understanding what would happen. Genesis states several times that Noah simply did what God had commanded him (Genesis 6:22, 7:5, and 7:16). Noah neither questioned nor complained. He is an early example of what Hebrews 11:1 says: "Now faith is the assurance of things hoped for, the conviction of things not seen."

Thus began the story of Noah and his relationship with God. I have wondered: Just how did God sound? How did Noah know it was God? These are questions that many of us have asked on our spiritual journey. Noah never described how he knew God's voice, but I sense that there was a different quality to God's voice than to the normal mind chatter. Not only is this a story about redemption and God's promise of safety; it is also a story about listening and the importance to listen for and follow God, regardless of how it may look to others. Let's begin by reviewing the story as it occurs in the Bible: Genesis 6–9.

Understanding the Story

God said to Noah, "I will establish my covenant with you; and you shall come into the ark, you, your sons, your wife, and your sons' wives with you" (Genesis 6:18). Right here, in this sentence is God's ever-present grace. Noah built the ark precisely as God commanded and followed God's instructions without any guarantee of what was to come. God, though, entered into an obligation with Noah and reaffirmed their covenant relationship.

The waters came and all was blotted out. It rained for forty days and forty nights (a biblical expression for "a long time"). It was unceasing. Noah remained faithful, and the day came when the rain stopped and the waters began to recede. In Genesis 8:4 we learn that the ark came to rest on the top of the mountain of Ararat in the seventh month of the seventeenth day of the month. There they stayed for several months until the waters receded and uncovered the land.

The day came when God told Noah to leave the ark with his family and all the animals. In gratitude Noah built an altar and offered a burnt sacrifice. While there was no commandment for Noah to initiate a sabbath, in Hebrew his name means "rest." Noah's initial action upon leaving the ark was to rest in God's presence and to have a holy moment of honoring all that had happened.

God blessed Noah and his family, and gave them the same instructions that the first human beings received—to be fruitful and multiply to fill the earth. In addition God gave the care of all the animals to this family and clarified the foods they were to eat and not eat. It was clear that the lifeblood of human beings was sacred and that no human blood should be shed. The penalty was that a murderer would be accountable to God.

God went another step and told Noah that there would be a sign of God's covenant with his family and all future inhabitants. It would be a rainbow set in the clouds. This rainbow was a reminder to God and every generation since Noah that never again will the waters become a flood that destroys all of life. God affirmed this in Genesis 8:21b–22: "I will never again curse the ground because of humankind, for the inclination of the human heart is evil from youth; nor will I ever again destroy every living creature as I have done. As long as the earth endures, seedtime and harvest, cold and heat, summer and winter, day and night, shall not cease."

WHAT DOES THE COVENANT SAY ABOUT NOAH?

Even though his life would not be what he had thought it would be, Noah was willing to listen to God. The determining factor in God's choice of Noah was his righteousness.[13] In other words, Noah and his family were the only ones who exhibited a strong moral fiber. One might wonder at God's unmerited grace towards Noah. Scholar John Gibson reminds us that "Noah is the first clear example in scripture of the man of faith who . . . goes God's way."[14] Noah walked with God not only during the building of that massive ark and through the possible ridicule of those who saw what he was doing, but also during the time spent drifting on the top of those flood waters and the months they waited on the summit of the mountain. Here was a faith so strong that in the face of mockery, and when fear may have overwhelmed them, when it seemed that the rain would go on forever, and then when it stopped, that the waters would never draw back, Noah kept doing what God asked him to do.

As the story goes (and we do not know if it is literal or figurative), "There were eight human survivors of the flood: Noah, his wife, their three sons (Shem, Ham, and Japheth), and their son's wives."[15] In many ways, they represent the new Adam and Eve family. Through Noah we can see "God the creator was at work among other peoples before Israel appeared."[16] In Genesis 9:1–7 we are told that God blessed Noah and his sons and told them that they were the beginning of something new. All human life is sanctified and has worth. Then in 9:8–17 there is a majestic statement about covenant that includes the whole of creation.[17] The covenant tells us that Noah was crucial in the redemption history of God.

WHAT ARE THE BLESSINGS AND CONDITIONS OF THIS COVENANT?

With this covenant, God initiated a new world and re-established a covenantal relationship with all living things. This was a unilateral divine covenant because "without anything on Noah's part—without any commitment, pledge, or guarantee—God obligated Himself."[18] God made an unconditional promise that would last forever. Through this divine covenant, we can see that God offered Noah, his wife, and all of their descendants new life, protection, and an irrevocable relationship with God. God will never cancel this bond. We, however, are free to walk away from it. It is our choice to act as if this, or any of the covenants, do not apply to us.

Throughout the Bible, we find the Israelites and the early Christians doing this very thing. They attempted to go out on their own or ignore the commandments given to them: most often with disastrous results. Even though the Israelites would turn from God time and again, the covenant with Noah would become an integral part of Israel's history, helping to define them as a unique tribal community, and later, as a nation among the other ancient civilizations.

The Covenant of Redemption and Safety builds on the Covenant of Care and Grace that God made with Adam and Eve. It is important to recognize that God does not revoke a previous covenant. It is enfolded and encompassed in each new covenant, as we see here in God's Covenant of Redemption and Safety with Noah. Today, we continue to receive the care and grace of the first covenant, while now knowing that we would also be safe forever from a completely destructive flood. In addition there was the blessing of redemption. This was God's special promise to humanity that our sins would not wipe us out if we live into God's covenant and accept God's grace and love.

One part of this blessing was that God willingly infused our lives with loving-kindness. The Hebrew word for this concept is *hesed* (sometimes spelled *chesed*). We have no comparable word in English. Yet, it "underpins the whole idea of covenant."[19] The closest we can come to this is to understand it as God's promise of unwavering faithfulness and steadfastness to us. God blesses us and remains loyal even when we are disloyal to God and how we have been called to live.

God's actions would be a blessing to humans, animals, and plants. Noah would have planted and tilled the land in order to feed his family. This mirrored the call God gave Adam to till the earth. In addition there would have been the blessing of vineyards and the advent of winemaking. In Israel's history, the vines, harvest, and wine all came to symbolize our connection to God and God continuing to give us life.

There were conditions with this covenant. Noah was to remain faithful in his care of the plants and animals. For instance, he was to eat only what was defined as edible by God. In caring for human existence, he was to have children, and to live in a community that covenanted together to follow God's commandments. We know that he fell short of this, as we do in our own lives and our walks with God.

An additional condition was that no human blood would be shed. This was an affirmation about human life and the call to value all people. In essence this was saying that we should not murder or harm one another. God told Noah that there would be severe consequences for violating this condition. God told Noah and his sons: "I will require a reckoning for human life" (Genesis 9:5b). God declared that those who kill another person will be directly accountable to God.

However, the flood did not eradicate sin from the world. In fact as the story of Noah continues we learn that he became drunk and this led to him being disrespected as he lay naked. Noah himself experienced the depth of God's grace, but he failed to extend grace to his youngest son Ham. He ended up cursing Ham while blessing the other two brothers. Noah's inability to forgive unfortunately set up a stage for future conflicts among his sons and their descendants (Genesis 9:20–27). So another condition, though, not stated directly, was to acknowledge our ongoing propensity to turn from God, and our need to seek ways to avoid temptations and sin.

In both the blessings and the conditions God is the subject, not human beings. God makes, God promises, God establishes—God is the one doing the acting. We are the recipients of this grace.

Understanding the Covenant's Relevance

WHAT DOES THIS COVENANT SAY TO US TODAY?

As I studied God's Covenant of Redemption and Safety, which God made with Noah and all future descendants, I continued to be amazed that in the wake of how destructive we can be to each other and to our environment, God always persists to show confidence in our desire and ability to live as God's people. Even though God's first inclination was to destroy all the earth and all of humankind, God found someone who was trustworthy and was willing to take a step back from the initial plan and give humanity a new beginning. What this says to me is that no matter how far we may stray from God, God never ceases to work in and through us.

We must be careful, though, and not think that this covenant means the earth cannot be destroyed. The rainbow does not cancel out our own ability to destroy what God has made through our irresponsibility with nuclear power and natural resources.[20] We are called, just as Adam and Eve were, just as Noah and his family were, to care for God's entire world. Clearly, this covenant speaks to the unity of all creation and reminds us of "all creation's total dependence upon God's active compassion."[21] If we are to remain faithful to this covenant, then we need to follow God's divine lead and recognize that we are the hands, eyes, feet, and ears on the scene. It is up to us to carry forth what God placed in front of Noah and thus we have an ongoing responsibility to care for all of creation, including the animal and plant kingdoms.

When we read this text carefully, we must note that it does not speak to a specific community of faith. It was not given to only one tribe or to a single nation. Even those who do not know of this covenant have experienced its effect in their lives up through today. Israel came to know God's promises through the oral history that was passed down from one generation to the next. They know that the promise was never to be kept as a secret for them to keep from others. Through Noah's story and God's covenant it is reaffirmed for all of us that it is in God's nature to save and to create. God called creation good in Genesis 1. This divine covenant is a reaffirmation of that statement. Even though the earth was destroyed, creation continued through rebirth and renewal of life.

HOW DOES THIS COVENANT INFORM
OUR CHRISTIAN DISCIPLESHIP?

This story can inform our faith and our walk as disciples and our life as a community of believers. When I first read this biblical account, I could not imagine being that faithful. I was in my late twenties and I thought that type of faith, exhibited by Noah, was only found in the Bible. At that time in my life, I worked in a hospital as director of intensive care and coronary care. This was part of my ten-year plan to become the youngest female hospital administrator in the country. I did not seek God's guidance because I believed that my plans were good and therefore I did not need the counsel. There was a lot of young adult arrogance in me. I had all the answers to life's questions, not only for me but also for my friends. So, I thought of this story as a good fable and nothing more; at least that is what I thought until my world and all of my plans were crushed by the changing circumstances of my life.

I had to leave nursing because of poor health. In the first few months, I flopped around like a fish out of water, slowly dying. One afternoon, a friend read to me this account and said, "Don't you think Noah and his family had plans that looked ruined forever?" The thought had never crossed my mind—of course that would have been true. But, at that point in time, there was no way I would have believed that it could apply to me because I did not see myself as part of God's ongoing story of creation and salvation.

Yet, you and I are part of this covenant. Kay Arthur writes that God "preserves you and me through the deluge of destruction, carrying us in His ark on the shoulders of His stormy waters while we lack for nothing."[22] Because of Noah's faithfulness, we are in the same covenant with God.

This entire story has meaning for us today. Through God's actions with Noah and his family, we can be assured that when God became bound to Noah it was with ties that could never be broken. God is not just our creator; God is also our protector and is involved and invested in us. This tells us that God desires to be in an intimate relationship with us and "we are to take seriously the biblical covenants God established with Adam, Noah, Abraham, David and through the baptism into Jesus' death and resurrection."[23]

This passage invites us to continuously reevaluate our relationship, not only with God and Jesus but also with each other. God showed us divine mercy when total destruction did not occur, even though it seemed humanity deserved it. This, alone, should inform how we are to interact with others who have wronged us. It can lead us to think differently about individuals and groups when we feel moved to act towards them as if they do not deserve any mercy. God's mercy, ultimately, extends to all of humanity—Jews and Gentiles, slaves and the free, rich and poor.

We can use this story as a mirror to evaluate our own preoccupation with self or with wanting others to meet our needs according to our wishes. When we remember that they, too, were called good and deemed worthwhile by God, then we should be able to view those we don't understand with respect and support. There is a power in this story that can help us be better disciples of Christ. When we see it not just as a good biblical tale, but also as a teaching tool for our lives, then our discipleship may radically transform.

Jane Ann Ferguson, in her pastoral perspective of Genesis 9:8–17, tells the story of a little boy who saw a rainbow and asked his mom, "Can we take it home?" This prompted the mother to write a poem called: "A Rainbow in My House." In her poem, she imagined the rainbow filling their home and shining so brightly that the house could not contain it.

As Ferguson mused about this poem she asked these questions: "What does the body of Christ look like in the light of a rainbow? What would it mean for a Christian community to put God's rainbow in their house?"[24] These are important questions for us to ponder.

As a pastor, I believe when we and our faith communities begin to see our churches shimmering in all the colors of the rainbow, we will be a witness to God's love and forgiveness in the midst of chaos; in the middle of pain and suffering. To be a faithful community of believers we are called to move out of our comfort zones and to ask: Who have we excluded from the ark? Do we want to leave out non-Christians? Those of a different ethnicity than ours? Homeless individuals and families? Hookers and pimps? Ex-cons? The mentally ill? Those who are Christian but have a different theology? Those with different lifestyles? As we grapple with these questions and seek God's directions, our faith communities will become places of justice. Justice in the sense of inclusion, of not leaving anyone out but welcoming the stranger, the orphan, those of all sexual orientations, people living with disabilities, the hungry, the poor, and the men and women released from prison.

The Christian church started as an open community. The Greek word for "church" is *ekklesia*. The early Christians did not create a brand new word for their faith community. Rather they adopted the term *ekklesia*, meaning "the Assembly," a well-known system that already existed in the Greek society. Athenian democracy was a direct democracy through which all citizens participated in the decision-making. At the heart of this democracy was *ekklesia*, in which "the decisions concerning major communal issues were taken in public by a simple majority . . . after open debate between all citizens who wished to participate."[25]

Was it merely coincidental that the early church used this term of the radical Athenian democracy for their spiritual community? I believe it was an intentional choice of early church leaders. By adopting such a term, they would have wanted to reflect that kind of an egalitarian, all-embracing, and welcoming community of faith. It also seems that the early church not only embodied the Greek democratic principle, but also even radicalized it all the more. In the Greek society, only citizens—free men—were allowed in the Assembly, thus automatically excluding women and slaves. Some early church writings indicate the vision of the Christian *ekklesia* to be a community where all people participate, as Galatians 3:28 so powerfully witnesses: "There is no longer Jew or Greek, there is no longer slave or free, there is no longer male and female; for all of you are one in Christ Jesus." At the same time, we notice that such a vision of an egalitarian community would have been at odds with patriarchal values demonstrated in a call for women to be silent in 1 Corinthians 14. It is humbling to recognize that our church leaders strove to include all God's people in the midst of conflicting values. We as the church still struggle to be a genuinely open and welcoming community, and to proclaim that today's ark is meant for all. In doing this we will discover the same redemption God gifted to Noah and his family.

Discipleship is defined in Merriam-Webster's dictionary as "one who accepts and assists in the spreading of the teachings of another."[26]* The central teaching of this covenant is one of God's love. It is important for every phase of our Christian journey. One of the profound messages of this story is that our hearts can be remade by God. Our churches can become "the ark," where we learn from both Noah and God about patience with each other, about broken hearts and healing, about renewal for our personal lives and our communities of faith. At the same time, the church must also resist the temptation to be sheltered in the ark. When the storms of injustice and oppression emerge, the ark might seem like a comfortable hideout. The challenge for the church is to actively engage in the rough waters of life, and step out of the ark, if it is needed.

As our hearts are broken open by God's immeasurable commitment to us, by God's unlimited mercy and grace, and God's willingness to show us how to start over again and again, the light of God that we will generate will force open the doors of our churches, and bust right through the walls, so that our churches will become places that everyone will want to be.

Noah shows us that there is no vision too big, nor a task beyond our capability to accomplish. There is that wise saying that with God everything is possible. We are called to take on God-sized dreams and God-sized tasks with the trust that, even if we do not know the first thing about how to achieve them, God will lead us if we will listen, trust, and obey.

This speaks to another way this story informs our discipleship and that is taking time to be in prayer. Noah could not have known what to do or when to do it if he had not been in deep communion with God.

It is through prayer that God can speak to us, and we can get insights to solve even the most complex problems. My mother, throughout her life, has used this technique to "hear" what God wants her to know. If she is troubled by something, or cannot solve a problem, she ends her day in prayer. At the end of that prayer she uses Samuel's line that the priest Eli told him to say, "Speak, Lord, for your servant is listening" (1 Samuel 3:9). Mom's experience is that

---

she sleeps soundly and with a deep peace. Most often she awakens early in the morning with the answer on her mind or the tension resolved.

John Wesley believed that it was only through prayer that ministers could minister and professing Christians could live a life that Jesus would call worthy. Prayer allows time for us to hear God's directions for our individual and community lives. Wesley felt that a group of Christians committed to prayer could accomplish any task God asked of them. He said, "I continue to dream and pray about a revival of holiness in our day that moves forth in mission and creates authentic community in which each person can be unleashed through the empowerment of the Spirit to fulfill God's creational intentions."[27]

Comparing the First Two Covenants

For us to compare the Covenant of Care and Grace (God's covenant with Adam) and the Covenant of Redemption and Safety (God's covenant with Noah), we must first recognize the similar elements in the covenants. According to Dr. Michael Fitch and Geoff Hawley in their book, *Covenants, Creation and Choice*, they identify eight characteristics of a covenant: It has a covenant holder. It is either bilateral or unilateral. It contains at least one promise from God. It often has conditions; something that was stipulated by God to be done or not done. It is in effect either for a limited time, or forever. It has a symbol or token that is a reminder for the people of faith or for God. It contains blessings and curses (consequences of keeping and breaking the covenant). Finally, it includes a covenant meal between the parties.[28]

While these elements are the most common ones, as we study other covenants we will discover that several were sealed in blood through a specific ritual. Rarely are all of these characteristics found in one covenant; this is a general guide.

WHO IS THE COVENANT HOLDER, AND IS IT BILATERAL OR UNILATERAL?

In the first covenant (Covenant of Care and Grace), the holder was God. Yet, it is considered to be a bilateral covenant because both parties—Adam and Eve, and God—professed their commitment to this divine covenant. Noah was the recipient of the divine covenant made by God. Therefore God, once again, was the covenant holder; but this one was unilateral. God did not seek Noah's agreement.

THE PROMISES AND THE CONDITIONS

For Adam the promise from God was that he and Eve would be fruitful and multiply. This same promise was given to Noah, his wife, their sons, and their wives. Likewise both were to take care of creation and love it as God loved it. Both were to till the earth. There was one major promise with Noah, as we have learned; God would never again destroy creation through a flood.

The conditions that led to needing to make the Covenant of Care and Grace with Adam and Eve were that they, both of them, disobeyed God's command to not eat of the fruit of the tree of knowledge of good and evil. It was all of humanity's sinfulness, with the exception of Noah, that led to God's decision to destroy all of creation. When God discovered one faithful family, God knew, at that point, that humanity would have the opportunity to begin again.

TIME FRAME THAT THE COVENANT WAS IN EFFECT AND THE SYMBOL USED TO SEAL THE COVENANT

The covenant with Adam and Eve is in effect for all eternity, and the covenant with Noah is viable for as long as the earth is in existence. The covenant with Adam was made initially at the time of creation and the symbol used was the Tree of Knowledge that remained in the center of the garden. Even after Adam and Eve were no longer in the Garden of Eden, the tree would be there forever as a reminder to God's people in every generation of the consequences of choosing to disobey God.

The token for the covenant God made with Noah was the rainbow. Yet, it is not only a reminder to humanity; it is also a reminder to God of the promise made to preserve creation and not destroy it with another flood.

THE BLESSINGS AND THE CURSES (CONSEQUENCES FOR KEEPING AND BREAKING THE COVENANT)

Prior to Adam and Eve eating the forbidden fruit, the blessing was that they had all their needs provided for; they did not need to plant or till. They were blessed to have an intimate relationship with God and to know God like no other human beings. There were severe consequences for their actions. Death and violence would now be a part of their lives—and ours—until Christ comes again and the kingdom comes on earth as it is in heaven.

Noah was blessed to be the chosen one to give humanity another chance. He and all of his family were blessed with the knowledge of how to do the work necessary to rebuild the earth. Since the covenant with Noah was unilateral, there were no consequences because it is not in God's nature to break a covenant.

THE COVENANT MEAL

The covenant meal with Adam and Eve was initiated with creation when the fruit-bearing trees and the plants that produced vegetables were created. This food was eaten in the context of their ongoing, personal, and "face-to-face" relationship with God. Noah, after the flood, created a prayerful time of worship where he sacrificed some of the animals. This is considered to be a seal of the covenant God made with Noah, though it was not required in this case.

In Genesis 9:3 God tells Noah and his family that everything that lives will be food for them. This was probably the first time meat would become part of the diet; since in Genesis 1:30 God said, "I have given every green plant for food." When Noah and his family ate their first meal on dry land this was a covenant meal with God and had the sense of a communion of thankfulness.

LOOKING AHEAD

As we move to our next chapter, a long time has passed in biblical history. The people, once again, turned away from their relationship with God and began living for themselves. The people even decided to build a tower tall enough to reach the heavens, which was not sanctioned by God. Their plans were thwarted by God, and their common language was confused so that they could no longer understand each other. This moved people out across the earth as they joined with those who spoke similarly, and various tribes were formed. Among the descendants of Shem (a son of Noah), in one of those tribes, was a man named Abram who had a wife named Sarai. They would be the next people God made a covenant with as another step towards our redemption.

Endnotes

1. Michelle A. Gonzalez, *Created in God's Image: An Introduction to Feminist Theological Anthropology* (Maryknoll, NY: Orbis Books, 2007), 4.

2. Ibid., 10.

3. Walter Brueggmann, *Genesis: Interpretation: A Bible Commentary for Teaching and Preaching* (Atlanta: John Knox Press, 1982), 13.

4. Chris Woodall, *Covenant: The Basis of God's Self-Disclosure* (Eugene, OR: Wipf & Stock, 2011), 2.

5. John C. L. Gibson, *The Daily Bible Study: Genesis*, vol. 1 (Philadelphia: Westminster Press, 1981), 101.

6. Ibid., 121.

7. Kevin J. Conner and Ken Malmin, *The Covenants: The Key to God's Relationship with Mankind* (Portland, OR: City Bible Publishing, 1983), 17.

8. For more on Desmond Tutu's theology of Ubuntu, see Michael Battle, *Reconciliation: The Ubuntu Theology of Desmond Tutu* (Cleveland: The Pilgrim Press, 1997).

9. Eleazar S. Fernandez, *Reimagining the Human: Theological Anthropology in Response to Systemic Evil* (St. Louis, MO: Chalice Press, 2004), 187.

10. Theodore Hiebert, "Episode 2 in *Creating the Covenant*," eds. Theodore Hiebert and Jaime Clark-Soles (Nashville: Abingdon Press, 2014), 15.

11. Kenneth L. Carder, *The United Methodist Way: Living Our Beliefs* (Nashville: Discipleship Resources, 2009), 53.

12. Brueggmann, *Genesis: Interpretation: A Bible Commentary for Teaching and Preaching*, 85.

13. Woodall, *Covenant: The Basis of God's Self-Disclosure*, 1, 8.

14. Gibson, *The Daily Bible Study: Genesis*, 1:189.

15. Woodall, *Covenant: The Basis of God's Self-Disclosure*, 8.

16. Terence E. Fretheim, "The Book of Genesis: Introduction, Commentary and Reflections," in *The New Interpreter's Bible* (Nasville: Abingdon Press, 2003), 395.

17. Brueggemann, *Genesis: Interpretation: A Bible Commentary for Teaching and Preaching*, 83.

18. Kay Arthur, *Our Covenant God: Living in the Security of His Unfailing Love* (Colorado Springs, CO: WaterBrook Press, 2003), 21.

19. Woodwall, *Covenant: The Basis of God's Self-Disclosure*, 12.

20. Fretheim, "The Book of Genesis: Introduction, Commentary and Reflections," in *The New Interpreter's Bible*, 401.

21. W. M. Lloyd Allen, "Genesis 9:8–17: A Theological Perspective," in *Feasting on the Word: Preaching the Revised Common Lectionary*, year B, vol. 2, eds. David L. Bartlett and Barbara Brown Taylor (Louisville: Westminster John Knox Press, 2008), 28.

22. Arthur, *Our Covenant God: Living in the Security of His Unfailing Love*, 21.

23. Ibid, 31.

24. Jane Ann Ferguson, "Genesis 9:8–17: A Pastoral Perspective," in *Feasting on the Word: Preaching the Revised Common Lectionary*, year B, vol. 2, eds. David L. Bartlett and Barbara Brown Taylor (Louisville: Westminster John Knox Press, 2008), 26.

25. Janet Coleman, *A History of Political Thought: From Ancient Greece to Early Christianity* (Malden, MA: Blackwell Publishers, 2000), 23.

26. *Merriam-Webster's Collegiate Dictionary,* 11th ed. (Springfield, MA: Merriam-Webster, 2003), s.v. "discipleship."

27. Pamela Rose Williams, "What Christians Want to Know: John Wesley Quotes: 23 Great Sayings," accessed December 30, 2015, www.whatchristianswanttoknow.com/john-wesley-quotes-23-great-sayings; original quote is from *How to Pray: The Best of John Wesley on Prayer* (Uhrichsville, OH: Barbour Publishing, Inc, 2008).

28. Dr. Michael Finch and Geoff Hawley, *Covenants, Creation and Choice: Where Theology and Science Overlap* (Bloomington, Indiana: WestBow Press, 2013), 58–59.

🔖 CHAPTER 3

The Covenant of Blessing

The entire story of the journey of Abraham and Sarah is found in Genesis 12–25. It is a great story with adventure, intrigue, revenge, deception, and sacrifice. Most of all it is a story about how God worked in and through these two flawed, yet faithful, human beings. It is our story for through it we can learn that our shortcomings will not turn God away. God has already blessed each one of us and, as with Abraham and Sarah, can use our mistakes and sins for good. This story tells us that God is never done with us. The foundational scripture that we will study is Genesis 15–17.

The call to Abram, whose name was changed by God to Abraham, occurs at the beginning of this story in Genesis 12:1 when the Lord said, "Go from your country and your kindred and your father's house to the land that I will show you." God told Abram that a great nation would come from him. Abram is puzzled. He and his wife are well beyond childbearing years. God in essence says that Abram does not need to try to figure it out. Through God anything is possible. So, Abram gave the order and everyone packed up and left. This was not just two people but the whole family, the servants, all of their animals, and their belongings. This was no easy task. It is hard to pack up everything and move when you know where you are going. Yet, Abram did not even know where God was going to send him; but he was faithful and obeyed.

The idea of obeying, especially obeying God, has been a difficult lesson for me to learn. Throughout most of my young adult life I rationalized why I did not need to pray and listen. How would I know it was God's voice? What if I followed some crazy notion in my head?

I battled with God about returning to church and then fought even harder when I felt led by God to become an ordained minister. Already, I was involved in social justice and had a wide network of friends. How could God want me to do anything different? I have wondered if Abram and Sarai thought the same thing. Did they question the sanity of leaving their native land and wandering off? Were they hoping that God would tell them when to stop? While those questions are not answered by our story in the Bible, we do know that they were obedient and continued on the journey.

When I finally answered God's call to enter the ministry, I felt led to attend Union Seminary in New York City. Once again, I fought God on that one. There was a good seminary right where I lived in Seattle, Washington. I decided to go there. God, though, would not leave me alone. It seemed that nothing at Seattle University's School of Theology and Ministry was as I expected it to be. "Stick it out," I told myself, because I never even wanted to visit New York City, let alone live there. I was only three weeks into the seminary that I had picked, when, in a moment of feeling lost and desperate, I filled out the application for Union. Secretly, I hoped I would not be accepted. I was. Reluctantly, I packed up and drove to what seemed like the other side of the universe.

With no exaggeration, the instant I pulled up to my new residence and walked into my room, a strange feeling swept over me: I felt as if I had come home. God had a plan for me but I needed to listen. God has a plan for each one of us and for our faith communities, just as there was a plan for Abram, Sarai, and the Israelites.

I was privileged to see this in action in a church community in Seattle. The pastor of this church had led the congregation into social justice. The time came when we were at a turning point. A needle exchange program came to the pastor and asked if there was a possibility to set up the program at the back entrance (which was down an alley). A small group of people began to research the pros and cons of supporting this program. To this group, it seemed that God was calling us to move in that direction. Yet, there were many questions and concerns, some of which could not be answered.

Finally, it was time to present our findings to the church council. Our hopes were not very high. We were shocked when supporting the needle exchange program passed on the first vote with a resounding yes. This step of faith took us on a journey to become a stronger community of disciples that continued to grow in its focus on justice and mercy; that first step led to many more yesses.

We discovered that as we opened ourselves to God, listened through prayer, and entered into holy conversations, we became more open to God's call on our community. This led to many unexpected blessings. Through this process, we realized that God gives us the wide brush strokes and we get to fill in the details. Abram and Sarai made mistakes, even some big ones and so will we. God, though, does not give up on any of us—ever. Pay close attention to the journey Abram and Sarai took when they said yes to God and to the covenant God made with them when their names were changed to Abraham and Sarah. More significantly, their lives were changed.

Understanding the Story

Abram was the son of Terah, who was a descendant of Shem (one of Noah's sons). Even with this lineage, Abram was an unlikely candidate to be selected by God. It is surprising to note that Abram's ancestors were actually idolaters.[1] In Joshua 24:2, the prophet said to all the people, "Thus says the Lord, the God of Israel: Long ago your ancestors—Terah and his sons Abraham and Nahor—lived beyond the Euphrates and served other gods." There was not much in Abram that merited God's choice of him. This was pure grace determined by God's will.

When Abraham and Sarah began their journey, their names were Abram, meaning "noble father," and Sarai, meaning "princess." When their names were changed by God, so were their identities. Abraham became the Father of Many (a Multitude) and Sarah, the Mother of Many Nations. It was a long journey. In the Bible their journey began in Genesis 12, and it was not until 17:5 that God gave them new names.

I imagine there were many discussions of turning back and times when their journey felt senseless and hopeless. Perhaps Abram might have wondered if he made it all up. Through it all, Abram and Sarai had just enough faith to keep going, and God was there beside them and making a way for them. God never left them. In fact, there were signposts that they were going in the right direction.

In Genesis 14:17–24 we read about Abram's meeting with King Melchizedek of Salem. Melchizedek's name means "righteousness" and Salem means "peace," making him the king of righteousness and peace. Melchizedek gave bread and wine to Abram and then blessed him. Some believe this was a foretaste of Jesus' covenant meal with his disciples.[2] Here, Abram was anointed. He was also reassured and given spiritual strength for the rest of his journey. One of the significant actions of Abram was that he gave a tithe to Melchizedek, one-tenth of his possessions. This would have been a considerable amount but Abram did not hesitate.

Months and years passed and Abram and Sarai did not see God fulfilling the promise of a son. The biological clock was ticking down and it seemed there was very little time left for God to do anything. What happened? Sarai came up with a plan and Abram agreed. They "figured out a way to 'help' God to fulfill the promise of fatherhood."[3]

Abram was just like many of us. We pray, we wait, we pray, and then when God does not respond according to our timetable, we begin to act on our own. Abram's alternative plan seemed reasonable; just as my plan to stay in Seattle for seminary seemed logical to me. It's similar to the first plan my church had for the needle exchange program, which was to help it find a better location. I thought my ideas would accomplish what God wanted me to do, just as the church council thought that moving the needle exchange away from the our building would be an acceptable alternative. Abram and Sarai thought the same thing about the idea of a surrogate son born by Hagar. We make it so much harder on ourselves by turning to our own devices rather than waiting on God.

Look at the grief both Sarai and Abram experienced over Hagar bearing the child, Ishmael, fathered by Abram. Think of the pain of humiliation that Hagar was forced to bear. All of this could have been avoided if Abram had not taken the reigns into his own hands. God, though, was still able to work in and through this mess to bring about the initial intention. A number of years passed before Sarai conceived, but she did. God kept the promise made to Abram.

God came to Abram in a dream in Genesis 15:12–20. It was at this point that God sealed the covenant with Abram. Each of these events emphasized God's light and love. God walked with Abram and Sarai, was there when they doubted, and stayed with them when they made wrong choices. God knew that right would prevail and that Abram and Sarai would be key components in God's redemption of humankind.

God made three covenantal promises to Abram: the promise of land, the promise of being the father of many nations, and a spiritual promise of being blessed. As with all covenants with God, God is the initiator. God establishes the covenantal boundaries, and states the conditions, and the curses and the blessings.

At the very beginning of the story of Abram and Sarai, God made an unbreakable pact with Abram. How did God make this covenant? What did God do? Did Abram or Sarai need to do anything? The answers to these questions will help us understand that we can give our whole lives and all of our possessions to God; we can become vulnerable enough to trust God in everything.

WHAT DOES THIS COVENANT SAY ABOUT ABRAM?

As this story begins, we find Abram has departed from Haran and journeyed to Canaan. At this point, there is no covenant. "There is no hint in scripture that the Lord entered into any covenant with him while he was in the land of Ur of Chaldean. Instead the land of Canaan was then set before him provisionally."[4] It was here, in Canaan, that God spoke to Abram and declared, "To your offspring I will give this land" (Genesis 12:7). Abram responded with gratefulness and an act of worship. Abram built an altar and continued the journey. When all of his family and servants reached Bethel, Abram once again built an altar and in thanksgiving invoked the name of the Lord.

Abram was filled with human flaws and at times was even disobedient. When they traveled to Egypt because of a famine in the land where they were, fear gripped Abram. He thought he would be killed if the Egyptians knew Sarai was his wife because of her beauty. He asked Sarai to tell the Egyptians that she was his sister. She did this when Pharaoh saw her loveliness and she became part of his harem. Abram was spared but his actions had consequences for Pharaoh, as God inflicted a plague upon his house for taking in Sarai. We do not know what Sarai went through, but can surmise it must have been a frightening time. Yet, Abram's actions did not lead to any enduring harm to his family or servants; even when Pharaoh discovered the truth. He simply sent them on their way. God continued to work with Abram's insecurities and fears to bring about God's desired results. Abram did not turn away from God but remained committed to accept God's directions.

God chose Abram, but Abram also chose God. This is the choice that each one of us has to make in our walk as disciples. Abram had to choose again and again to walk with God every time he took matters into his own hands and seemed to turn from God's direction.

Our covenant-making God shows us that when Abram said yes, the mighty and miraculous happened. "All Hebrew history begins with Abraham. He is the great ancestor of the Jews and holds the place of honor as their father. . . . All God's dealings with Israel—past, present and future—are rooted in the Abrahamic Covenant."[5] This could not have happened without Abram's consent.

Abram demonstrated two dominant spiritual characteristics: He obeyed and he believed God. Over and over again, throughout the Bible, we hear these words—obey and believe. It is not always easy and, as we read in this story, it was not straightforward for Abram. He did not "possess any mysterious spiritual secrets that are hidden from us."[6] God showed Abram all he needed to know, and God has told us all we need to know. It was Abram's obedience and faithfulness that allowed God to continue working in and through him. Abram became a mighty channel of God's grace. He was initially a person who worshiped many gods; he was not a mighty warrior; nor did he possess any other superior powers. Abram, in many ways, was like you and me. Yet, God made a covenant with him, and Abram led his people to a new beginning. "He obeyed and, moving in a world of unseen realities, he ventured into eternal greatness in his Covenant-God."[7]

It cannot be stressed too much that Abram and Sarai are you and me. This covenant, as are all of the divine covenants, is a part of us. They are important in our understanding of faith and the call God puts on each heart. But, like Abram and Sarai, we have to say yes in order for God to use us. Far too many times, as a pastor, I have heard, "I will teach Sunday school after my youngest graduates from high school." "I will go on a mission trip when I have enough money." "I cannot become a minister, a deaconess, a home missioner now; maybe later." "I don't care if God wants me to give a sermon; it is never going to happen." "I don't have the skills to do that." "That is not something I enjoy." "We, the church, cannot afford it." "God could not want us to do that!" "Let me put it to you, plain and simple: It will not work."

Abram and Sarai could have said many of the same things. It was not the right time for them to leave—maybe the crops were just about to come in, or it was calving time. They could have thought they did not have enough resources to take everyone and everything with them. Perhaps they felt unprepared for such a journey. Excuses probably abounded everywhere. However, Abram did not let those thoughts cloud his recognition that this God, who called him to a seemingly impossible task, would not only show him the way but supply all of the travel needs for everyone.

The God who appeared to Abram is the same God who sent Jesus and the same God who created us, claims us, and calls us to our own greatness.

WHAT ARE THE BLESSINGS AND CONDITIONS OF THIS COVENANT?

Even before a covenant is made, God blesses Abram and Sarai as they are getting ready to leave their country and his father's home. God says, "I will make you a great nation, and I will bless you, and make your name great, so that you will be a blessing. I will bless those who bless you, and the one who curses you I will curse; and in you all the families of the earth shall be blessed" (Genesis 12:2–3). Just a few verses later, in Genesis 12:7, the Lord appeared to Abram after they went through the land of Canaan to Shechem and stopped at the oak of Moreh where the Lord said to Abram: "To your offspring I will give this land."

Blessing is the central point of God's covenant with Abram. There was the personal blessing God gave to Abram. This was, in essence, when God anointed him and, through this action, all who believed in Abram would have realized that he had found favor with God. We are never told that anyone else heard God's voice, or recognized God's presence. Part of the blessing was that others were willing to follow Abram, just as Noah's family had been willing to get in an ark without understanding what would happen.

In the story we find this personal blessing playing out when Abram receives the bread and wine from Melchizedek along with his verbal sanction. Later, in Genesis, Chapter 13, we find the blessing of property fulfilled in the lives of Isaac and Jacob, and finally all of Israel. All of these blessings transformed both Abram and Sarai; this is why God eventually gave them their new names of Abraham and Sarah.

Through Abram's obedience to God a river of blessing poured out to the people and to the land. Abram was not only blessed, but he was also to be a blessing. There is a saying, "What you put into the world will always come back to you." Abram did not hold on tightly and become possessive of God's blessings to him and his family. He was generous to others and in turn they blessed him and were blessed by God. One way we see Abram blessing others was in his generosity to Lot in allowing him to choose his land and in rescuing him from Sodom (Genesis 15:6–9; 14:1–16; 18:16–33).[8]

It is important to note that Abram did not fully understand what was expected of him or what God wanted him to do. Just like us, Abram must have wondered how he would know if all God said was true, especially when there was no son in sight. Abram wanted a tangible sign from God. "God assured Abram that he had understood correctly, and that the inheritance would, in the first instance, be received by members of his own 'natural' line."[9] God took Abram outside and had him look to the heavens and count all the stars. God said, "If you are able count them. . . . So shall your descendants be" (Genesis 15:5). In that moment Abram believed the Lord, but God was not done.

The blessings and God's commitment were sealed in the act of covenant making found in Genesis 15:6–12; 17–18. This rite symbolized an oath of life. Theologian and scholar John Gibson reminds us that "the ceremony which he [Abraham] partially prepared and partially witnessed in a vision was not a sacrifice but a rite to ratify a solemn agreement."[10] God was the only one who walked through the animals, so this was a unilateral everlasting covenant initiated and ratified only by God. This covenant was not based on Abram's worthiness. Abram was not asked if he accepted the covenant, but it "was the sign he had craved."[11] His willingness to obey led him, Sarai, and the Israelites to become the recipients of the blessings in this covenant; thus it is the Covenant of Grace.

With this covenant Abram became Abraham and Sarai became Sarah, and it signifies a new life of covenant living. It is important to note that the conditions of this covenant were not dependent on Abraham's past, present, or future good works. There was nothing he could do that would diminish or increase what God had already promised.

God told Abraham that he and all of his offspring would keep this covenant in every generation. The covenant was sealed by God's directive: "Every male among you shall be circumcised. You shall circumcise the flesh of your foreskins, and it shall be a sign of the covenant between me and you" (Genesis 17:10–11). God instructed Abraham that not only was this covenant for his heirs but it also extended to the servants he bought and those born in his house.

Blood was shed again; this time on the part of all those associated with Abraham; and it was a sign/symbol of God's covenant with them. Circumcision was an outward symbol of their inward commitment to God and a demonstration to the world of this commitment. This rite was passed down from generation to generation. Still, today, for our Jewish sisters and brothers it is a vivid and visual reminder of what God told the father of the Israelites.

Therefore, it is understandable that circumcision was at the heart of the controversy in the early church as the Christian community grew beyond the Jewish circle. The question was whether the new converts to Christianity needed to be circumcised. When Peter was accused of eating with the uncircumcised, he powerfully witnessed that the Spirit instructed him not to make distinction between the circumcised and the uncircumcised (Acts 11:1–18). Eventually, the church leaders met in Jerusalem and decided that circumcision was no longer a mandate (Acts 15, Galatians 2). This decision did not in any way revoke the Abrahamic covenant but expanded the everlasting aspect of this covenant by finding its power not in the physical body but in the heart of the believer (Romans 2:29). They utilized an idea that already existed in Judaism: "Circumcise, then, the foreskin of your heart, and do not be stubborn any longer" (Deuteronomy 10:16). The circumcision of the heart was not only for Jewish males anymore but also for women, those of different ethnic backgrounds, and all who longed to have a relationship with God. Abraham's covenant reflected God's boundless love.

It is critical to understand that, just as with Noah, this covenant was not limited to blood heirs. This was also a spiritual covenant that extended to those who even Abraham and Sarah might have considered unworthy—their servants from other tribes who held different beliefs. As with the rainbow, the sign of circumcision points to something greater. The permanence and irreversibility of circumcision can be seen as a symbol of God's unconditional and irrevocable promise. The rainbow and the rite of circumcision are signs to help us remember how God has acted in the past, and has helped to direct our lives in the present toward God and continue the work that was called for in these covenants.

Abraham and Sarah were not told of any direct curses or consequences that would come from them becoming covenant breakers. The curse was towards anyone who did not believe and denied the truth of what God did through Abraham and Sarah. God did not give a list of tasks that needed to be accomplished. "What God wanted from Abraham was his dedication, to walk before Him and be blameless, something Abraham, being human, did not always do."[12] Yet, when he made mistakes he did not turn away from God and God did not decide to choose someone else. Overall, Abraham was faithful and obedient. These two qualities made him a conduit of God's grace for all generations.

Understanding the Covenant's Relevance

WHAT DOES THIS COVENANT SAY TO US TODAY?

Abram, Sarai, Lot, and the entire family and their servants all left a place they knew. They left behind security, friends, the familiar, and the place they called home. On one level this makes absolutely no sense. They did not have any assurance that God would do what God said. Until that time, Abram was from a family that worshiped many gods. Yet, something in him responded, much like the disciples did when Jesus called their names and said "Come follow me." They, too, had no knowledge of where they were going or what they were going to do. The only fact they had was that a man called Jesus touched their souls and they had to learn more.

The Covenant of Blessing demonstrates to us that Abram's trust in God's voice led to a desire for him to seek out this God by following God's directions.

He, in essence, wanted to learn more about the God who called him and his family to be leaders/representatives for this God. Abram was not always faithful, as we have studied. Yet, his unfaithfulness did not lead him to quit, to turn around and to go home. In spite of doubts, Abram continued to believe in the Lord. He continued to take steps forward even when all the evidence was contrary. There was one overarching theme to Abram's faith: He believed that God had something wonderful in store for him. Walter Brueggemann describes Abram's acceptance of God's directions as "an act of faith."[13]

I cannot stress enough how important it is for us to understand this covenant in relation to our world today. We live in difficult times and to many it seems as if God is nowhere to be found. One person came to me after a sermon and said, "Pastor Evy, I think that God is just sitting back waiting for us to destroy ourselves." When I asked how he came to that conclusion he responded: "If God was here, don't you think that more of us would take a stand against all the violence and hatred; all the rhetoric that leads us to be so fearful of each other?"

We have the choice to embrace radical change just as Abram and Sarai did, or continue on and do what we have always done. This Covenant of Blessing puts some critical questions in front of us:

1. What does it mean to be a community of faithfulness?
2. Where is God calling you to challenge the status quo?
3. Where has your faith community become stuck?
4. What risks need to be taken to move in a new direction?
5. How can those with a vision be more supported when not everyone sees it?
6. What is needed to trust God's promises to always be with us, and give us the wisdom and courage to move into new territories?

Answers to these questions may not be easy. Yet, as we keep questioning and exploring, we may be led to new insights.

This covenant reminds us that God's promises are for eternity, not just a specific time or a certain group of people. God's promises and blessings to Abram are promises and blessings to us today. It also tells us that we have to take the steps to walk with God. God is not going to pick us up and turn us around; we have to say yes and then follow.

In the midst of seemingly uncrossable gulfs that divide groups of people, this story stands in the middle as a reminder that in our human struggles, our doubts, and even our questioning of God, there is a way. As a commentary points out, "Hope and humanity are held in tension throughout this passage. On one hand we are permitted to identify with Abram's human struggle and desire for confirmation of the promise made to him; on the other, we are called to mimic his response in verse 6 [Genesis chapter 15]: Abram believed!"[14]

For Christians, one of the major ways this text can inform our lives as individuals and as communities is to fully embrace the fact that God has not given up on us, just as God never gave up on Abram. Therefore, we should not give up on God. The world we know may seem like it is breaking apart, and we may desperately attempt to keep it the way we have always known it to be or want it to be. We might take things into our own hands much like Sarai and Abram. We do this when we forget that God still acts in our world and that God's timing is not our timing. Let us learn from Abram and Sarai that there is nothing so difficult in our present circumstances that God cannot work through it to bring us to a new place and a fresh start in life. Our task is to learn how to be faithful in the best of times and in the worst of times.

HOW DOES THIS COVENANT INFORM OUR CHRISTIAN DISCIPLESHIP?

As individuals: Throughout the Second Testament we find many references to Abraham. He is remembered in Hebrews 11 where the writer first tells us that "faith is the assurance of things hoped for, the conviction of things not seen." This was a hallmark of Abram and Sarai's journey. These words are also a touchstone for each one of us. For Abram to become Abraham and Sarai to become Sarah did not mean they never questioned God; in fact they did that often. What it took was their willingness to continue despite their doubts and questions.

This text from Hebrews 11:1 is important in my personal journey. When I was in the middle of my seminary education, I began to question my call. I was not seeing any fruits of my labors; though I am not sure I even knew what I was looking for except more affirmation that I was on the right course. My actions mirrored those of Sarai and Abram when they decided to take things into their own hands. I began to look for a different avenue of ministry, one that was outside of the church. I found something that excited me, and I made a tentative commitment to take a new direction in my life. I called for an appointment with the dean of students so that I could alter my course of study. But literally the night before our meeting I had a dream.

In that dream, it was dark and I was on an empty and lonely street lit only by a couple of lamps. Suddenly, I heard a sound. It startled me and I began running. The sound came closer. I ran faster to get away from it. As it was about to overtake me I heard a voice and it said, "Are you going to keep running or will you let me lead?" The dream ended with me standing in the street crying. Immediately I woke up and knew that what I had heard was the voice of God. I realized that, once again, I wanted to run the show, determine what was to happen in the future, and take the steps toward what I thought God should do in my life. I needed to place God back in charge and pray for clarity and courage. It only took a few days for me to know that my plans were not God's plans. If I was to stay on course, God needed to be the driver. Even though I had complicated my life in ways that would not have happened if I had trusted God, God led me through the mess and, with minimal consequences, I was back on track.

I needed the faith of Abram and Sarai to continue on, no matter how things looked; especially when there are no obvious signs from God. And like Sarai and Abram, if I had been open to any signal from God that I was headed in the right direction, in time I might have recognized it.

As a community: These same words from Hebrews 11:1 speak to our larger faith communities. It was not just Abram and Sarai on a journey; it was their family and their community. Abram, in particular, was the leader of all of them and was the one who made the choice to move forward even though he did not know where they were to go. When has your faith community been asked to make a change and did not know where it would lead? What were the difficulties? The fears?

There had to be difficult times, tensions and moments when some of those with Abram wanted to leave; perhaps many did. To follow God as Abram and Sarai did is not easy; yet, when we say yes, we step into the Covenant of Blessing.

Our faith communities can be stopped, though, from saying yes to God because of impatience and/or thinking that God is either absent or does not act fast enough. These are common characteristics of our culture and of our Christian churches. We want what we want when we want it and, many times, do not even stop to pray and listen. As disciples we can learn from Abram and Sarai that God will act, but it will be on God's timetable. The question for us is, will we remain faithful when nothing seems to be happening or we do not have clarity about our next step?

In Hebrews 11:8–16 the writer spells out all that happened to Abram because of his faith, and because of the promise of an inheritance that was greater than he could ever imagine. He and his immediate family died before all the promises God made to Abram were fulfilled, but God kept those promises and remained in covenant with each subsequent generation.

Our discipleship journey is no different than what we have studied thus far. Just like Abram and Sarai, there are times when God is silent and that calls for us to be more diligent about our practices, not less. Instead of deciding that prayer or Bible study does not work and is not helping, the silence is an invitation to keep praying, keep studying, despite evidence that "tells" us it does no good. We are to keep doing what Jesus calls us to do and to believe as he said in John 14:12 that "the one who believes in me will also do the works that I do and, in fact, will do greater works than these." In addition we are to pray earnestly; and to not just look for the results we expect or want.

We are called to be the church. *The Book of Discipline of The United Methodist Church* clarifies that: "This mission is our grace-filled response to the Reign of God . . . God's grace is active everywhere. . . . It is expressed in God's covenant with Abraham and Sarah, in the Exodus of Israel from Egypt, and in the ministry of the prophets."[15] Our church is not for ourselves. Kenneth Carder, retired United Methodist bishop, reminds us "that the church belongs to God and not to us. The church is to be present in the world on behalf of the God by whose grace it has been called into existence."[16]

In Romans 4, Paul writes to the people of his day, and to us today, about the example of Abraham. This passage helps us to understand that God's covenant was not just with the people of Israel. Abraham was blessed by God before the act of circumcision. Paul writes, "He received the sign of circumcision as a seal of the righteousness that he had by faith while he was still uncircumcised" (Romans 4:11).

This lets us know that, just as with Noah, the story of Abraham has additional implications for us as we acknowledge the reality that we live in a multifaith world. Our own *Book of Discipline* tells us that "as we make disciples, we respect persons of all religious faiths and we defend religious freedom for all persons."[17] We can ignore this to our peril, or see that in these two covenants God has cast a wide net. Noah and his family repopulated the earth and there was no command that they have a central unified belief. With Abram the blessings of land and descendants as numerous as the stars occurred before the covenant ritual and before the seal of the covenant. Paul wrote, "and the scripture, foreseeing that God would justify the Gentiles by faith, declared the gospel beforehand to Abraham, saying, 'All the Gentiles shall be blessed in you.' For this reason, those who believe are blessed with Abraham who believed" (Galatians 3:8–9).

The religious pluralism of our world presents us with both gifts and challenges. It is when we truly learn to live in harmony with one another in the midst of many faiths that our world will be a more peaceful place to be.

For Paul, our faith does not give us the right to insist that we deserve God's blessings or grace. As a disciple this is important to understand because we have a tendency to think that faith equals favors. Here in God's covenant with Abram, we see that God's gracious actions came before Abram acted in a certain way or met specific requirements. In fact, God's grace led to Abram's faith and the new journey signified by his new name Abraham.

Ephesians 2:8–9 reminds us that "for by grace you have been saved through faith, and this is not your own doing; it is the gift of God—not the result of works, so that no one may boast." Paul tied these words to Abram's journey for the followers in Ephesus. He was reminding them that their works would not guarantee God's blessings, that all they had were already gifts from God. As disciples, it is easy for us to get caught up in the belief that what we have obtained in the world is due to our hard work and has nothing to do with God. I had an older gentleman tell me one day, "I don't give to church because it is my money and I can do with it what I please. So I don't care how much you tell me I should give, I am not going to do it unless I decide to spend what I have made in that way." At the other extreme, there have been several individuals whom I have met in my ministry that repeatedly made it known to me just how much they have given and how much they do for the church. They expected praise and special attention. We each need to be honest about where we stand on the continuum between these two points of view.

Once again, we can look to Abram and Sarai and note that neither of them declared that any of the blessings from God were an outcome of their faith or their good deeds. In our walk with Christ, we need to keep our eye on who is the mover of the heavens and earth, and be careful to not seek credit, but rather give credit to God.

However, "Like Abram, we can question God as part of our faithfulness and trust. We also live expectantly that God's promises of life, hope and future are extended to us in Jesus Christ . . . who calls us to take the next step and follow him."[18] The divine covenants are for all, down through the ages.

Comparing the Covenant of Blessing with the First Two Covenants

Walter Brueggemann in *The Covenanted Self: Explorations in Law and Covenant* writes that there are three levels of covenanting: the first level is with God, the second level is with neighbor, and the third level is with self. In the covenants with Adam, Noah, and Abram, all three levels were present. First, God initiated the covenant, and each had the choice to follow or ignore what God was doing. Second, the neighbors were primarily their family members. In addition, Adam was given the responsibility of caring for all creation. Similarly, Noah took in animals as his neighbors and cared for them in the ark. Abram's neighbors included those he met along the way. Third, each one at times broke the relationship with God and self. Adam disobeyed God. Noah was consumed by drink. Abram was dishonest. Yet, they were restored into a right relationship.

God's covenant with Abram contained many of the elements that were previously defined in Chapter 2. Each covenant has its own unique characteristics, but there are many similarities.

WHO IS THE COVENANT HOLDER, AND IS IT BILATERAL OR UNILATERAL?

As with the covenant with Adam, the covenant with Abram is considered to be a bilateral covenant. God was, as always, the covenant maker, but Abram was the one who set up the altar for the sealing of the covenant. He, in essence, agreed to participate in this ritual. According to Fitch and Hawley, "To enter into a covenant the following steps must be taken; first to hear it, second to accept it, third to believe it and fourth to act upon it."[19] Adam, Noah, and Abram took these exact steps.

THE PROMISES AND CONDITIONS

We can begin to see how the covenants include and build on the previous ones. From Adam where God promised to fill the earth, to Abram where God tells him that his descendants will be as numerous as the stars, we find God enlarging the scope with each covenant. Here, as we have learned, God promised Abram land and descendants that would continue. There was one condition, though: that Abram "walk before God [faithfully] and be blameless."[20] God stated this condition clearly after Abram and Sarai had shown that they occasionally doubted God's ability to act. No other conditions were given.

TIME FRAME THE COVENANT WAS IN EFFECT AND THE SYMBOL USED TO SEAL THE COVENANT

Here, the covenant with Abram, like the one with Adam, is considered to be eternal. This covenant would continue through all of Abram's descendants. "Its oath was given to Isaac and it was confirmed to Jacob and then to Israel after him (1 Chronicles 16:15–17)."[21] The covenant with Abram was sealed by the act of circumcision. This was a bloodletting which left a mark. Abram may have been aware that the act of shedding blood between human covenantal partners was a sign of it being eternally sealed, because theologian Peter Golding reminds us that "the covenant concept was familiar to Abraham's contemporaries (and probably had been for some generations earlier)."[22] This was not a one-time act, since every male that was descended from Abram was to reenact this ritual. It was a way for everyone to remember not only what God had done, but also what

God had promised. And it was a call for each male to be like Abram and to faithfully walk with God.

THE BLESSINGS AND THE CURSES (CONSEQUENCES FOR KEEPING AND BREAKING THE COVENANT)

We know the blessings of the covenant with Abram: land and descendants. What about the curses? No curses were explicitly spelled out, but we can see the consequences of disobeying this covenant God made with Abram. God clearly said that those who blessed Abram would be blessed and those who cursed Abram would be cursed.

THE COVENANT MEAL

When Abram met Melchizedek, the priest of the Most High God and a king of righteousness and peace, he offered Abram bread and wine, and then bestowed a blessing upon him. Even though these actions occurred in Chapter 14, and the actual making of the covenant did not happen until Chapter 15, this was considered to be the shared meal, since Melchizedek was God's representative. Jesus was said to be a priest in the order of Melchizedek (Hebrews 7:17).

LOOKING AHEAD

After Sarah and Abraham had Isaac, Abraham married Keturah who bore him six more sons. It was only, Isaac, though, who carried the blessings of God forward. Isaac had twin sons, Esau and Jacob. Jacob continued to be a channel of the blessings God gave to Abraham (his grandfather), and Jacob had twelve sons who became the leaders of the twelve tribes of Israel. Over time, these tribes were to become a nation, and the next covenant was made with Moses at Mt. Sinai after the exodus of the Hebrew people who were descendants of the twelve tribes. This covenant is "based on the Abrahamic Covenant [the Covenant of Blessing] and is an outgrowth and further development of that covenant."[23]

As we study God's covenant with Moses, the Covenant of Guidance and Law to live by, pay particular attention to how this covenant differs from the previous three. In this, God is establishing a relationship with a nation, rather than just with an individual.

Endnotes

1. Arthur W. Pink, *The Divine Covenants* (Memphis: Bottom of the Hill Publishing, 2011), 67.

2. Kevin J. Conner and Ken Malmin, *The Covenants: The Key to God's Relationship with Mankind* (Portland, OR: City Bible Publishing, 1983), 35.

3. Kay Arthur, *Our Covenant God: Living in the Security of His Unfailing Love* (Colorado Springs, CO: WaterBrook Press, 1999), 28.

4. Pink, *The Divine Covenants*, 72.

5. Guy Duty, *God's Covenants and Our Time* (Minneapolis: Bethany Fellowship, Inc., 1964), 17.

6. Ibid, 19.

7. Ibid.

8. Conner and Malmin, *The Covenants: The Key to God's Relationship with Mankind*, 29.

9. Chris Woodall, *Covenant: The Basis of God's Self-Disclosure* (Eugene, OR: Wipf & Stock, 2011), 20.

10. John C. L. Gibson, *The Daily Study Bible Series: Genesis,* vol. 2 (Edinburgh, Scotland: The Saint Andrew Press, 1982), 54.

11. Ibid, 55.

12. J. Maurice Wright, *God's Covenant Plan: Living in Him* (Maitland, FL: Xulon Press, 2011), 83.

13. Walter Brueggemann, *Genesis: Interpretation: A Bible Commentary for Teaching and Preaching* (Louisville: John Knox Press, 1982), 144.

14. Kenyatta R. Gilbert, "Genesis 15:1–12, 17–18: A Homiletical Perspective," in *Feasting on the Word: Preaching the Revised Common Lectionary*, year C, vol. 2, eds. David L. Bartlett and Barbara Brown Taylor (Louisville: Westminster John Knox Press, 2008), 53.

15. *The Book of Discipline of The United Methodist Church*, "The Mission and Ministry of the Church," ¶121 (Nashville: Abingdon Press, 2012), 91–92.

16. Kenneth Carder, *The United Methodist Way: Living Our Beliefs: The Revised Edition*, (Nashville: Discipleship Resources, 2013), 122.

17. Ibid.

18. Daniel M. Debevoise, "Genesis 15:1–12, 17–18: A Theological Perspective," in *Feasting on the Word: Preaching the Revised Common Lectionary*, year C, vol. 2, eds. David L. Bartlett and Barbara Brown Taylor (Louisville: Westminster John Knox Press, 2008), 54.

19. Dr. Michael Finch and Geoff Hawley, *Covenants, Creation and Choice: Where Theology and Science Overlap* (Bloomington, IN: WestBow Press, 2013), 55.

20. Ibid, 58.

21. Conner and Malmin, *The Covenants: The Key to God's Relationship with Mankind*, 28.

22. Peter Golding, *Covenant Theology: The Key of Theology in Reformed Thought and Tradition* (Scotland, UK: Christian Focus Publications, Ltd., 2004), 71.

23. Duty, *God's Covenants and Our Time*, 25.

 CHAPTER 4

The Covenant of Guidance and Law

To understand the significance of God's covenant with Moses and the Israelites, we need to have some background information. In the covenant with Abraham, one of the promises was of land. This promise, though, would not be fulfilled until many generations later. Isaac, Abraham's son, also received the same blessings from God, which were extended to his son Jacob. There was a long and convoluted history before the promise of land would be achieved, including the many years that Abraham's descendants lived in Egypt. At first they were welcomed there, but that changed over the years and they were made slaves. It is important to understand what led the Israelites to slavery, because this is where the covenant with Moses begins. It is also critical to note that in the experiences of injustice and oppression under the Egyptian imperial rule, the Hebrew people came to know God as the one who would bring freedom and liberation to suffering people.

Briefly, Joseph was the favorite son of Jacob. His brothers were jealous and sold him into slavery, but they tricked their father into thinking he had been killed. This story can be found in Genesis 37.

In Egypt, Joseph remained faithful to God; yet, he still made a name for himself in a foreign land. He rose into prominence, and when a famine hit all the surrounding countries Joseph had secured enough food for Egypt. Jacob's family did not have enough to eat and in a dream God told Jacob to not be afraid of going to Egypt to obtain food for the family. It was with great trepidation that Jacob sent all of his sons except the youngest, Benjamin, to see if it was true that Egypt had food and would allow them to move there. In a wonderful story that spans four chapters in Genesis, chapters 42–45, Joseph becomes reunited with his family. For generations, they prospered in Egypt but the time came when a new pharaoh no longer remembered Joseph and all he had done. By this time, the Israelites had grown to a great number and the Egyptians became fearful that they would soon outnumber them. This irrational fear led the pharaoh to enslave the Israelites and order all the male children of the Israelites to be killed. Moses, one of those children, was placed in a reed basket by his mother in an attempt to save him. He was rescued by the pharaoh's daughter. This is the beginning of our covenant-making God coming to the Israelites to secure their release.

Put yourself in the shoes of the Israelites; they would have told stories of their ancestors, how great they were, and how successful they had been in Egypt. They would have lamented over their fate of being enslaved. In those many, many years of slavery, it must have seemed that God had abandoned them.

Moses, himself, had a complicated history. He grew up in the palace, as a member of the royal family. We do not know how he learned of his heritage, but he did. He was a grown man when he killed an Egyptian who was beating a Hebrew slave. After this incident, his life was in jeopardy and so he fled from Egypt and went to Midian where he settled down and married.

It was during that time that "the Israelites groaned under their slavery, and cried out. Out of the slavery their cry for help rose up to God. God heard their groaning, and God remembered his covenant with Abraham, Isaac, and Jacob. God looked upon the Israelites, and God took notice of them" (Exodus 2:23b–25). It was in response to this gross suffering of people that God acted to engage in history. God's liberating and saving actions revealed in the events of Exodus and the covenant making in the wilderness would eventually become a defining aspect of the Hebrew faith. Thus the stage was set for the time when God would make the Covenant of Guidance and Law with the Israelites. The foundational scripture for this covenant is found in Deuteronomy 9–11, Exodus 19–20, and Leviticus 25.

Understanding the Story

Moses, like Noah and Abraham, was quietly going about his daily tasks when suddenly life took an unexpected turn. Abraham, Noah, and Moses were not extraordinary people. They had not prayed to God for a special anointing. It was God who chose them for a specific job at a specific time. Their tasks were neither easy nor simple; they took years, or generations, to complete.

Moses was out tending his father-in-law's flock of sheep on what seemed like an ordinary day when suddenly out of nowhere "the angel of the Lord appeared to him in a flame of fire out of a bush; he looked, and the bush was blazing, yet it was not consumed. Then Moses said, 'I must turn aside and look at this great sight, and see why the bush is not burned up.' When the Lord saw that he had turned aside to see, God called to him out of the bush, 'Moses, Moses!' And he said, 'Here I am'" (Exodus 3:2–4).

God declared who God was to Moses and relayed that he, Moses, was to be God's representative to the pharaoh to bring release of the Israelite captives from slavery. Our compassionate God heard the suffering cries of the Israelites and was moved to act on behalf of the whole community. God chose Moses to be the one to lead God's people to a new land. God still hears our cries. In situations of political oppression, economic hardship, military confrontation, and all kinds of prejudices and discriminations, the cries of people in agony are taken to the very heart of our loving God. The Exodus story is a symbol of hope for suffering people and communities. Our liberating God challenges us not to lose hope today.

God's call for liberation may come to us as a surprise. Nothing could have been further from Moses' mind: liberating his people was something he did not think he could do. He found many excuses. Moses felt unworthy, exclaiming, "But who am I?" He was filled with fear when he asked, "But what if they don't believe me?" and he felt ill-equipped, and reminded God that he was "slow of speech and tongue" (Exodus 4). God was not going to let him back down. For each excuse, God had an answer.

Unable to dissuade God, Moses obeyed and, along with his wife and sons, left Midian to return to Egypt. All of them must have felt some fear at the prospect of this journey. Yet, God gave Moses a sense of assurance. Aaron, Moses brother, met him along the way and became Moses' spokesperson, but it was Moses who carried the power of God with him.

On their journey back to Egypt, Moses taught Aaron all God had told him to say and showed him the signs given to him by God. Upon their return they gathered the people, and Aaron repeated Moses words and demonstrated the signs from their God. The people believed, bowed down, and worshiped. This began their journey out of Egypt to the place where God would make a covenant with them.

WHAT DOES MAKING THIS COVENANT SAY ABOUT MOSES?

There was one unique and special quality that Moses exhibited. He was passionate about justice. Three times before his call from God, Moses responded to what he thought was an injustice. According to Rabbi Evan Moffic, Moses demonstrated his desire for fairness by:

1. **Defending the oppressed:** Moses' first act as an adult is defending an Israelite slave. He leaves the palace and sees an Egyptian taskmaster beating a helpless slave. Moses intervenes and stops the beating. *For Moses justice does not differentiate between slave and master.* Even if the master had a legal right to beat the slave, he did not have a moral one.

2. **Doing what's right, even if it meant criticizing his own people:** The next time we see Moses is when he encounters two Hebrew slaves fighting with one another. He does not turn away and ignore it because they are his people. He intervenes and chastises the one who instigated the fight, showing he is not afraid of criticism and making enemies. *He will do what is right in every circumstance.*

3. **Remaining faithful wherever he was:** After Moses is forced to flee Egypt, he arrives in the land of Midian. His first stop is a well. There he encounters a gang of shepherds harassing a group of seven sisters seeking to water their flock. Moses intervenes, defending the sisters. He is a stranger in a strange land, yet he does not shy away from seeking justice.[1]

God probably could have chosen someone else who would not have given so many excuses. However, God observed what Moses had done in the face of adversity. God needed someone who would keep standing up for the people of Israel no matter what the opposition. While we admire Moses' faithfulness and leadership, we must also note that his action of violence in killing the taskmaster is not to be justified.

As we have studied, Moses did not easily accept this very difficult assignment from God. He wanted to avoid it; he tried to convince God that he was not the right person. How many times has one of us done that same thing? I remember vividly when I thought I had a call to ministry. No way was I going to say yes. I was doing work to make people's lives better and I had absolutely no desire to be a minister. But like a pebble in my shoe, the idea of ministry continued to rub my consciousness. I gave all my excuses: I am too old. I do not need to go back to school. I do not want to be ordained. I have a disability. I am a woman, and too short for the pulpit. Some of my excuses were serious and others just plain silly. Yet, for me to even think about ministry as a possibility for my life, God had to squelch my doubts. I was just like Moses.

My objections were silenced by an amazing Spirit-filled woman named Viola. In the midst of my confusion, I returned for a visit to my hometown, Omaha, Nebraska. While there I called Viola and told her that I was exploring the possibility of going to seminary. I asked her out to lunch to get her advice. Once we both arrived at the restaurant and were settled in, her first words were: "So tell me why you think you have a call?" I shared with her several experiences. We were not even done with our main course when she stood up, slapped her hands on the table and asked, "Well, girl are you going to answer the call or not?' I replied with a meek yes. Still standing, she hit the table with both hands again and said, "Well, good, the conversation has ended." She turned, looked back, winked at me, and left.

Like Moses, I needed some nudging, prompting, and encouragement. As I studied the story of Moses, I reflected on how I almost did not follow God's call. I wonder how close Moses came to remaining in Midian. His yes set in motion events and a history that impact our walk as disciples today. The covenant God made with Moses, which we have come to know as the Ten Commandments, gave structure to the spiritual, social, and political life of the Israelites. As we study the covenant, keep in mind that it

> . . . is the most complicated and most difficult of all covenants to interpret. The elaborate wording of the covenant, the prolific and intricate details of the sacrifices, priesthood and sanctuary, and the complete governing of the national life of Israel by Sabbaths and religious festivals make it the fullest expression of a covenant in scripture.[2]

Understanding the Covenant, Its Blessings and Conditions

From the moment Moses received God's call to return to Egypt, God was in a covenantal relationship with him. It may not have been sealed in blood, there may not have been a covenant meal, but Moses was under God's guidance and care. Moses "would turn Israel back to God and deliver them from Egyptian bondage. This deliverance was based on the covenant of grace and faith made with their fathers, Abraham, Isaac and Jacob."[3] God says to Moses in Exodus 3:15–16: "Thus you shall say to the Israelites, 'The Lord, the God of your ancestors, the God of Abraham, the God of Isaac, and the God of Jacob, has sent me to you': This is my name forever, and this my title for all generations." God declared that the covenant-making, covenant-keeping, and covenant-equipping God had not wavered.

God's assignment went beyond Moses' ability and his confidence. He needed Aaron, his brother, and God's assurance through signs and frequent nudging to keep him on track when he waivered. What a lesson for all of us. When any one of us spearheads a project in our faith community it is easy to fall into the trap of, "I am the leader, therefore, I need to do this by myself. No one else is as capable as me." Clearly, Moses did not think this way. He did not accomplish this great task by his own strength, his knowledge, or even his own perseverance. He knew that if left to do it by himself, failure was guaranteed. As with the other covenantal stories, we find that trust in God, even in the face of absolute uncertainty, was once again a key component of faith. Moses embodied this trust, especially when the Israelites questioned him and turned against him. He kept going back to God, bringing the challenges he faced, the desires of the Israelites, and his own insecurities.

It took an amazing amount of perseverance to just get the Israelites out of captivity. Exodus 7:11–11:4 is the story of the ten plagues. After each of the first nine plagues, Moses was met with failure. His people were still in captivity. Each time, God told him to go back to Pharaoh and issue another warning. It was not until the death of all the first-born Egyptians that the cry from the Egyptian people themselves led to the release of the Israelites.

The journey did not get any easier. The Israelites found themselves wandering in the desert where they encountered fear, thirst, hunger, and hopelessness. In each instance Moses went to God, and God answered their need. We need to ask ourselves, what is the reading on our barometer of trust? Is it high, hovering in the middle, not quite trusting, or low, causing us to abandon a task or a direction God is leading us in? Moses returned to God, again and again, when it would have been easier to succumb to the cries of the people who wanted to go back to Egypt and to slavery, but he knew that God would not let them down.

Their journey finally brought them to the base of Mt. Sinai. It was here that God created the covenant, not just with Moses, but also with the Israelites who would later become a nation. While the covenant with Moses is covered in Exodus 19, much of the First Testament through Numbers, and other books of the Bible, some specific references can be found in the following scriptures:

- The Ten Commandments (Exodus 20:1–21, Deuteronomy 5:1–21)
- The Law, which is distinct from the commandments, fulfilling the covenant with Abraham (most of Deuteronomy 29 plus Exodus 19:5–16)
- The Levitical priesthood (Deuteronomy 18:1–5)
- The tokens of the tablets of stone and the designation "sabbath" as a day of rest where no work should be done (Exodus 31:18 and Leviticus 23:3)
- The ratification by blood and oath (Zechariah 9:11 and Deuteronomy 29:12)[4]
- The Sabbath Year (Leviticus 25:1–7)
- The Year of Jubilee (Leviticus 25:8–17)

According to theologian Owen J. Brandy, it took more than one trip up the mountain for Moses to receive all that God wanted to teach them. Moses had to make at least seven trips. Each trek required endurance and stamina: Yet, for the sake of the Israelites, Moses made every one of them. The first time Moses went up the mountain, God made the covenantal offer. God said to Moses; "Now, therefore, if you obey my voice and keep my covenant, you shall be my treasured possession out of all the peoples" (Exodus 19:5). God also told Moses that they would become a kingdom of priests and a holy nation. All God wanted was that in their hearts they would desire the same thing. When Moses returned and told them all God had said, then "the people all answered as one: 'Everything that the Lord has spoken we will do'" (Exodus 19:8).

They said the right words, but it would be a long time before they were willing to live them out. A friend of mine, Beth, has talked about her call to ministry. She says that when she was fourteen, while at a United Methodist summer camp, she felt certain that God had tapped her shoulder and whispered,

"You are to be a minister." Beth stood up in front of the group and declared her call, and gave her answer, "Yes, I will." It was another twenty years before she took the first steps towards fulfilling her words.

In one church where I was a lay leader, the community had come to consensus that they were called to feed and clothe the hungry right outside the doors. At first there were a lot of fear-filled voices: "We can't afford it." "It's too dangerous." "What if we fail?" Yet, a small group kept the fires of this commitment burning. Nearly seven years after the initial vision, a shelter with showers, a washer and dryer, mailboxes, and assistance for job interviews began to emerge. There were many challenges and some wanted to stop and go back to what was familiar. Their dream, though, was continually guided by the Holy Spirit and eventually it came to full fruition.

We are the Israelites and they are us. We share doubt, fear, going back on our word, while also sharing a deep knowing that we have been named and claimed by a grace-filled God.

Moses went back up the mountain. God told him to go back down and prepare the people. Moses sanctified them with a specific ritual and let them know that the presence of God would arrive in their midst. Moses obeyed and God called him back up. (I do not know about you, but I wonder how many treks I would be willing to make.) This time God told him to warn the people not to approach God or cross over the boundary.

> As Moses returns down the mountain, the people waited with bated breath. He reemphasizes the necessity to approach this encounter with a reverent heart. Then without warning, God begins to speak (Exodus 20:1). At that point, God speaks from Mt. Sinai with His voice the words of the 'covenant' that people of all faiths recognize as the Ten Commandments. The trembling people listen in stunned silence until God finishes.[5]

The people became fearful, not filled with awe at the fact that God spoke to them, but scared of what they had encountered. No longer did they want

God to talk to them directly. They had a choice to be ruled by their fear or to bow down in reverential awe. They chose fear, and pleaded for Moses to listen to God on their behalf and then tell them what God said. God, though, was already in a covenantal relationship with these people. All they needed to do was to acknowledge that and live in the way God would direct them. "What is conditional upon obedience is not the making of the covenant but the enjoyment of the blessing which the covenant contemplates."[6]

Moses went back and forth up and down the mountain five more times. The first time he brought down the Ten Commandments on the two stone tablets, panic once again had overtaken the people, and under Aaron's watch they had built a golden calf as an altar. They were ready to worship whichever god they thought would keep them safe and alive. "And the fact that they were acting out of fear should help us understand why they had no power to resist the temptation to fall into the sin of idolatry."[7]

Moses had to plead with God to not destroy the people because they had sinned and built an idol to worship. God relented and agreed but they would be held accountable. Unfortunately, when Moses returned to his people and saw the calf, he became so angry that he threw the tablets down and they shattered. God ordered the people to leave the camp, but God still kept watch over them.

In Exodus 34, the two tablets are reissued. One last time, Moses went up the mountain and returned again with the tablets of laws to guide them in becoming a great nation. Interestingly, "Archeology has revealed that contracts between two nations were sometimes written on two identical tablets of stone, with the same text on each. The stones would be arranged back to back and placed so that the join between them was set upon the boundary between the two nations."[8] Once again, God used a symbol that the people would have recognized. In Exodus 32 we learn that Moses carried down two tablets with words written on the front and the back. Symbolically, when arranged together they can represent the boundary between heaven and earth.[9]

God renewed the covenant by saying, "I hereby make a covenant. Before all your people I will perform marvels, such as have not been performed in all the earth or in any nation; and all the people among whom you live shall see the work of the Lord; for it is an awesome thing that I will do with you. Observe what I command you today" (Exodus 34:10–11).

The Ten Commandments are but one part of the covenant God made with the Israelites. These utterances are part of the moral code, and are at the heart of "the elaborate system of divine laws set out in the books of Exodus, Deuteronomy, and Numbers. In late antiquity, Judaic scholars organized the laws into 613 commandments."[10] Chris Woodall, theologian, identifies three distinctive categories in the Mosaic law: the moral law, which is reflected in the Ten Commandments; the civil law, which has to do with how the Israelites were to treat the alien, the widow, the orphan, and the servant; and the ceremonial law, which are the feasts and festivals designed to celebrate and give thanks for God's grace and goodness.[11]

A section of the moral law is found in Leviticus 25, and addresses environmental and economic justice. In Leviticus 25:3–4 the Lord says to Moses, "Six years you shall sow your field . . . but in the seventh year there shall be a sabbath of complete rest for the land." Then, in Leviticus 25:8–10 God says:

> You shall count off seven weeks of years, seven times seven years, so that the period of seven weeks of years gives forty-nine years. Then you shall have the trumpet sounded loud: on the tenth day of the seventh month—on the day of atonement . . . And you shall hallow the fiftieth year and you shall proclaim liberty throughout the land to all its inhabitants. It shall be a jubilee for you; you shall return, every one of you, to your property, and every one of you to your family.

Theologian George A. F. Knight reminds us that "this chapter [Leviticus 25] has some very important things to say to us today."[12] "What we should recognize," he goes on to say, "is that it was the spirit of God's commands that was to be observed as changes in Israel's social life kept taking place. There was still another great change coming in Christ. But the spirit of God's law stood unchanged. The reason: God is the same yesterday, today, and forever."[13] The spirit of God's law includes the responsibility to care for and not exploit the marginalized, the equitable distribution of resources, and the prevention of gross inequality.

Both of these laws were to function as restoration. The first is to restore the land so that it could continue to give grain and grapes. The second is based on God's call for us to have the opportunity at renewal, to begin again. Together we find that these laws emphasize:

1. Liberty for all.
2. Complete relaxation offered to everyone so that families might be reunited in joy and contentment. (A man could even reclaim his ancestral property at this jubilee.)
3. Freedom for all growing things to recover their natural cycle of life.[14]

GOD'S INTENTION

The covenant procured through Moses was not for himself, but for the emerging nation of Israel. God wanted the chosen people of Israel to come together as a faithful nation, with the Covenant of Guidance and Law as the framework, which would keep them in a righteous relationship with God and with each other. God showed them through Moses "how they were expected to conduct themselves in worship, at work, and in the life in community, all instructions revolving around the essence of covenant—relationship."[15]

Through Moses, God elaborated on a theme that was present in the previous covenants. It is encapsulated in the Hebrew word *hesed*. We first explored this word in relation to God's covenant with Noah where it was used to convey goodness or loving-kindness. Now, "Moses uses it in the sense of unfailing love."[16] God's intention is for the people of God to embrace the truth of God's steadfast love that we encounter time and again as is seen in each of the covenants.

THE ACT OF GOD MAKING THE COVENANT
OF GUIDANCE AND LAW

Long before Exodus 34, when God reaffirmed the covenant, the covenant was established with Moses and the seventy-five leaders of Israel. This occurred in Exodus 24. There, we find the two traditional elements of covenant making: sealed in blood and a common meal. In this chapter we learn that Moses had verbally given to the people of Israel what would later become the Ten Commandments written in stone. They agreed to follow what Moses relayed from God, but, as we learned, they responded from their fear of what would happen if they did not agree. Fear would never lead to following God, only love. Even so, the covenant was ratified. Moses set up twelve stones to represent the twelve tribes of Israel. Moses then sacrificed the appropriate animals and sprinkled the blood upon the altar and over the people. This sealed the covenant with the entire community. Following that, the leaders (seventy elders plus Moses, Joshua, Aaron, Nahab, and Abihu) ate a covenant meal and then God summoned them up the mountain to meet together.

No matter what the people did, they could not destroy the covenant God made with them. No matter how far they strayed off course, the covenants were there to lead them back, just as they are there for us. In Chapter 6, we will come to understand how Jesus is the representative of God in the everlasting covenant that is unwavering, and unbreakable. God is with us, as God was with Adam and Eve, Abraham, Noah, Moses, and David. In this covenant with Moses and the ancient Israelites, we see how determined God is to show us the way to be in right relationship with God and with each other. The Israelites only had to obey and they would receive the blessings of God, and the same holds true for us through Christ Jesus. Blessings do not always mean that we will receive what we desire. Rather, God's blessings indicate that God will be with us always to strengthen and guide us even in the most challenging times in life. At times God may seem silent and absent, even though we cry out for help with our most earnest faithfulness and prayers. As the Israelites had to wander in the wilderness for a long time, we too may need to wait until God responds to us in God's own time. In the meantime, we are to trust in God's steadfast love.

THE BLESSINGS FOR KEEPING THE COVENANT
AND CURSES (CONSEQUENCES) FOR BREAKING IT

The blessings for keeping this covenant are clearly spelled out in Deuteronomy 28 where God tells the Israelites that if they obey, their nation will prosper and "all these blessings will come upon you and overtake you." Their blessings will be too numerous to count, as they will find themselves blessed whether they live in the city or the country. Enemies will flee and all people of the earth shall know that they are called by God. There is only one stipulation—that they diligently obey all the commandments from God (Deuteronomy 28:14).

This same chapter definitively lays out the curses or consequences for disobeying the word of God. All of the blessings will become curses, so that crops will fail; cities will struggle and crumble; the people will experience more panic and difficulty in everything they attempt; rain shall become dust; their animals shall die; and they will be conquered by their enemies. The consequences go on and on for fifty-three verses. One would think that understanding what will happen to them if they turn away would be enough to keep them on track and to seek God quickly when they have sinned. Yet, that was not true for them, as it seems to be for us. Even the Apostle Paul speaks of this in Romans 7:15 where he writes: "For I do not do what I want, but I do the very thing I hate." Probably every one of us has a story about how we did something we knew was wrong and paid the consequences for it.

God called the Israelites, and us today, to not blindly obey, but to listen to God, and let our love for God lead us to do what is right in God's eyes. I had a powerful and unforgettable lesson of not responding when called by God to care for the poor. It was a blustery winter day in Seattle, Washington, where the damp, cold wind chilled you to the bone. My friend Monica and I were doing some Christmas shopping at Best Buy. Out of the corner of my eye I saw two young boys, maybe six and eight, holding hands and quietly walking around the store. They were dressed in only flimsy t-shirts and shorts. Their feet were bare. Suddenly, a store clerk stomped up to them and in a loud voice said, "Get out of here, you do not belong in this store." Immediately, these words formed in my throat, "Oh, there you are, I have been looking all over for you." However they remained unspoken as I watched them leave. Fear of what the clerk would say, or maybe do, kept me silent. When I realized what I had not done, I ran out of the store to find them in order to buy them some warm clothes and maybe a meal; but it was too late. Those two beautiful children of God had disappeared into the dark coldness of late afternoon. My consequence has been the regret I have felt all of these years. God has worked with that regret to show me how to respond in the moment of need. While I was not cursed in the biblical sense, I certainly missed a blessing.

In our church communities our reluctance to begin a new program, our fear of failure or perceived economic loss can lead us to turn from a path God calls us to walk. When we do this, we miss out on blessings that we could not have imagined. Within every faith community there are these stories. But, also, the glorious times when we have discovered, again, the path that leads us to do what is right in God's eyes.

HOW DOES THIS COVENANT
BUILD ON THE PREVIOUS ONES?

From the beginning, God had a plan. God worked with a lineage and then a nation that, through their covenants with God, would be a blessing to all of humanity (Exodus 19:5; Romans 2:11). Adam and Eve received a new beginning and inheritance. Noah and his family were saved from the flood and, once again, repopulated the earth, caring for all of creation. Abraham and Sarah left Ur of the Chaldees, followed God, and received the blessing of a son who would be of the lineage leading to Joseph, Jesus' earthly father. Moses led the Israelites out of bondage to the edges of the Promised Land and received the laws by which they would be a civil and caring society.

There is a strong connection to the Covenant of Blessing with Abraham. God told Moses that he was "The God of Abraham" (Exodus 3:6). Moses would have understood this in covenant terms. So, the covenant with Moses was built on this foundation, which gave the laws through which the promise and blessings of Abraham would not only be fulfilled, but also extended into the full community of Israel and finally into the world. "The Mosaic Covenant [Covenant of Guidance and Law] did not annul nor replace the promises of the Abrahamic Covenant . . . The Mosaic Covenant was added to or 'placed alongside' the Abrahamic Covenant."[17]

All of the covenants presented, thus far, inform us about the nature of God. God will offer a way to begin again. God did not turn away from the first humans when they disobeyed, and God gave new possibilities for humanity when all seemed lost, as told through the covenant with Noah. God's covenant with Abraham and Sarah tells us that even when we believe there is no way, God makes the impossible become possible. Together these covenants and the final two tell the story of how God cares for us, acts with and through us, and will continue to unveil ways to live as God's people.

Understanding the Covenant's Relevance

WHAT DOES THIS COVENANT SAY TO US TODAY?

It is common in some circles of Christian thinking to believe that Jesus abolished the laws set forth in the First Testament. Theologian and reformer John Calvin reminded the people of his day and us today that these commandments continue to show us how to live before our God and with our neighbor; they give us solid advice in maintaining ourselves as a civil society; and that these commandments are essential for our Christian life.[18] They are a light for us, a spiritual light, not telling us what we should do to receive God's grace, but reminding us how people who claim to be disciples should live because they have the free grace offered to them by God through Christ Jesus. George A. F. Knight tells us that "the theology of the New Testament cannot be different from the theology of the Old Testament."[19]

Remember how it seemed that all the Israelites were involved in the creation of the golden calf because they were afraid Moses would never return? I imagine that there were some who did not feel that way, but felt it was easier to go with the majority than to speak out. This story is a reminder that we too can be led away from Jesus' true teachings when we surrender to the voices that say something quite different. God's grace is always available to help us choose faithfully, as well as to lead us back when we go astray. We can use the covenant with Moses and the Ten Commandments to help guide us to find or rediscover the social and spiritual commandments that came from these laws and which were lived out in Jesus.

HOW DOES THIS COVENANT INFORM OUR CHRISTIAN DISCIPLESHIP?

Walter Brueggemann speaks to our walk as disciples in relationship to the Covenant of Guidance and Law in his book *The Covenanted Self: Explorations in Law and Covenant*. He writes about God's commandments as "disciplines essential to the revolution."[20] This is a summons for us as Jews and Christians to create a social revolution where the world is marked by justice, mercy, and peace. Moses in his day, and Jesus in his, were both subverting the common customs and practices that defined some people as "in" and others as "out."

When we study the Second Testament we find that all the covenants are an integral part of it. In the Gospels, we see that Moses was part of the Transfiguration, where the disciples Peter, James, and John experienced a holy moment with Moses, Elijah, and Jesus. In Galatians 5, Paul guides us to understand that the Ten Commandments help us to identify sin, but says we are not to follow them in a legalistic sense but rather be led by the Holy Spirit in the way to embody these commandments as Christ's disciples.

As people of God, the first four commandments show us how to love God for God's own sake, not because God did something for us. The next commandments give us the directions for how to be a good neighbor and develop a caring community. Jesus said, "I have not come to abolish the law but to fulfill it" (Matthew 5:17); he was and is the only one who consistently keeps all the commandments. He is our teacher and model on how to embrace the stranger (wanted or unwanted), how to care for those who are poor, and how to love everyone equally.

This covenant is central to Jesus' life and his teachings. His great commandment was to love God with all our heart, mind, and soul and to love our neighbor as ourselves. As Christians, the Ten Commandments offer us a blueprint for actualizing Jesus' words.

In addition, in Leviticus 25 and throughout the Mosaic Covenant we can find instructions on how we are to be involved in economic and environmental justice. For instance, our call is not to just take from the land but to see how our actions can lead to destruction of the ecosystems of life that were created by God. To follow this directive, we need to explore how to let the land, rivers, and oceans recover. As faith communities we need to seriously wrestle with the values and guidelines found in this covenant.

Defining environmental issues as a theological problem, theologian Sallie McFague challenges churches to become better stewards of God's creation. She suggests a call to action for Christian communities to become ecological, take public stands on environmental justice, and pay attention to God's deep concern for the whole creation. According to McFague, human beings cannot thrive apart from nature, for salvation means "the flourishing of all God's creatures," not just human beings.[21] As McFague presents the importance of linking theology and the environment, she discusses a "communitarian view of human beings," in which our human life is inseparably linked to all living things.[22]

The Social Principles of The United Methodist Church call on us as individuals and communities to respect all of God's creation—the natural world, the world community and its people, and the economic systems. The simple yet profound message is that "all creation is the Lord's, and we are responsible for the ways in which we use and abuse it."[23] As communities of God's created world, we are called to make necessary changes in economic, political, social, and technological conditions to support a more ecologically sustainable world for all of God's creation. Living out the covenant today must mean far more than celebrating Earth Day once a year. We must overcome our anthropocentric focus in worship, preaching, education, and church programs, and always have the big picture of God's whole creation in mind in all that we do as God's people.

Environmental justice is closely related to economic justice. One of the economic justice recommendations in the Bible is the Year of the Jubilee. The instruction was not only to return the land taken for payment of debts but also extended into fair ways to enter into agreements. It was not that the powerful shall take and the poor shall give. This was a time to rebalance the scales and to start anew. If we followed this principle, the wealth inequality we now experience would be considerably lessened. There were instructions on care of the widow, the orphan, and the stranger. These were individuals who would be unable to secure employment or have enough means for food and housing. It was also the time of rest for farm animals and land. The covenant, especially in Exodus 20:22–23:33, gives expectations of behavior towards such matters as slavery, wise stewardship, giving accurate testimony, as well as guidelines for work and worship. How can we in our faith communities work to restore the imbalances between those who have more than enough and those who can barely survive? Pointing to the growing gap of global wealth distribution, theologian Elizabeth A. Johnson reminds us that our God is the God of liberation and calls us to practice justice, "Naming God the liberator does not just craft one more symbol to add to the treasury of divine images. It puts a question mark next to every other idea of God that ignores the very concrete suffering of peoples due to economic, social, and politically structured deprivation."[24]

Johnson emphasizes that "praxis of justice" is needed not just in the places of poverty and suffering, but also in the worldwide church. She especially challenges "the complacency of Christians in the affluent countries of the Northern and Western Hemispheres," and asserts the need to "take responsibility for our participation in the institutional and structural injustice in the global economy."[25] The covenant is a way through which God gives us direction to be a just and equitable society. Jubilee and other economic aspects of the covenant guide us to prevent gross wealth inequality.

John Wesley declared that his followers were not only to "assist the poor by offering food and clothing but also by education. He built a school . . . with a large hall for preaching, facilities for two school-masters. . . . He was especially concerned that the poor children not only learn to read, write, and cast accounts, but more specifically, to know God and Christ Jesus."[26]

Wesley's sense of social justice is part of the foundation upon which Methodism was built. If we are to follow his example, then our Christian discipleship needs to focus on restoring social-economic justice such as Leviticus 25 spells out, as Jesus taught, and as Wesley exemplified in ways that were appropriate for his time.

Comparing the Covenant of Guidance and Law with the First Three Covenants

We have learned that each covenant does not stand alone, but is in alignment with and builds on the previous covenants. The Covenant of Guidance and Law is no exception. God who gave Adam and Noah a way to start over, and who chose Abraham to be the father of the people who would become the nation of Israel, chose Moses as the person to lead the twelve tribes into nationhood. Each covenant is embedded in and expanded on by the previous ones.

WHO IS THE COVENANT HOLDER AND IS IT BILATERAL OR UNILATERAL?

This is the first instance where the covenant was made with a group of people instead of a single person. God chose Moses to be the representative for the whole body of people. The Covenant of Guidance and Law is for a group to follow, not just the individual it was made with. This covenant is bilateral in that God initiated it, but Moses had to receive it and agree to take it to the people. It is interesting to note that the leaders of the people participated in the seal of blood and the covenant meal, and, thus, everyone agreed to follow it.

THE PROMISES AND CONDITIONS

The main promises of God were to bring the people to a land that would be secured for them, and to bless them in every aspect of their lives. There was only one over-arching condition and that was to obey and follow the laws perfectly. This included celebrating the prescribed religious festivals.

THE BLESSINGS FOR KEEPING THE COVENANT AND THE CURSES (CONSEQUENCES) FOR BREAKING IT

The blessings, as we have studied, were extended to every aspect of the Israelites' lives, just as the consequences for not following the law as given by God and relayed by Moses extended to all. Most scholars agree that while there were many curses, again for each aspect of life, the final one was the destruction of Israel if the people did not repent and come back to God.[27]

THE COVENANT MEAL

Once again, as with the other three, there was a covenant meal. This one occurred in the presence of God, with all the leaders of the Israelites. The significance of this is that it is the first time more than one person participated in the sealing of the covenant through a meal. The leaders were also present when the covenant was sealed in the blood ritual.

LOOKING AHEAD

As we begin the study of the fourth covenant, the Covenant of Eternal Rule, we will not only read about God's divine covenant with David, who became king; we will also learn about the covenant between David and Jonathan, King Saul's son. This is the only major biblical covenant that was established between two individuals. It is important because it contains elements of Jesus' covenant with us.

Endnotes

1. Rabbi Evan Moffic, "Three Reasons God Chose Moses," accessed September 19, 2015, www.rabbimoffic.com/god-choose-moses.

2. Kevin J. Conner and Ken Malmin, *The Covenants: The Key to God's Relationship with Mankind* (Portland, OR: City Bible Publishing, 1983), 40.

3. Ibid., 41.

4. Dr. Michael Finch and Geoff Hawley, *Covenants, Creation and Choice: Where Theology and Science Overlap* (Bloomington, Indiana: WestBow Press, 2013), 71.

5. Owen J. Bandy, *The Glory and the Covenants: The Old and New Covenants According to the Apostle Paul* (Outskirts Press, Inc., Denver, CO), 2009, 12.

6. Peter Golding, *Covenant Theology: The Key of Theology in Reformed Thought and Tradition* (Christian Focus Publications, Ltd: Scotland, 2004), 93.

7. Bandy, *The Glory and the Covenants: The Old and New Covenants According to the Apostle Paul*, 15.

8. Finch and Hawley, *Covenants, Creation and Choice: Where Theology and Science Overlap*, 72.

9. Ibid.

10. Chris Woodall, *Covenant: The Basis of God's Self-Disclosure* (Eugene, OR: Wipf & Stock, 2011), 23.

11. Ibid.

12. George A. F. Knight, *The Daily Study Bible Series: Leviticus* (Philadelphia: The Westminster Press, 1981), 149.

13. Ibid., 150.

14. Ibid., 152.

15. Woodall, *Covenant: The Basis of God's Self-Disclosure*, 21.

16. Ibid., 22.

17. Conner and Malmin, *The Covenants: The Key to God's Relationship with Mankind*, 42.

18. George W. Stroup, "Exodus 20:1–17: A Theological Perspective," in *Feasting on the Word: Preaching the Revised Common Lectionary*, year B, vol. 2, eds. David L. Bartlett and Barbara Brown Taylor (Louisville: Westminster John Knox Press, 2008), 76.

19. Knight, *The Daily Bible Study: Leviticus*, 153.

20. Walter Brueggmann, *The Covenanted Self: Explorations in Law and Covenant* (Minneapolis: Fortress Press, 1999), 38.

21. Sallie McFague, *A New Climate for Theology: God, the World, and Global Warming* (Minneapolis: Fortress Press, 2008), 32.

22. Ibid.

23. *The Book of Discipline of the United Methodist Church*, "The Natural World," ¶160I (Nashville: Abingdon Press, 2012), 105.

24. Elizabeth A. Johnson, *Quest for the Living God: Mapping Frontiers in the Theology of God* (New York: The Continuum International Publishing Group, Inc., 2008), 86.

25. Ibid.

26. Richard P. Heitzenrater, *Wesley and the People Called Methodists* (Nashville: Abingdon Press, 1995), 105.

27. Finch and Hawley, *Covenants, Creation and Choice: Where Theology and Science Overlap*, 58.

CHAPTER 5

The Covenant of Eternal Rule

This chapter is unique in that we will study not only God's divine covenant with David, but also a covenant made between two men: David and Jonathan. Remember that the First Testament covenants "mark the principal stages in the development of God's purpose of mercy toward our fallen race. Each one brought to light some further aspect of truth. . . . The covenants and the history are so intimately related that some knowledge of the one is indispensable to understanding the other."[1] While all the previous covenants are incorporated into the Everlasting Covenant that God made with us through Christ Jesus, the two covenants in this chapter are foundational for us to understand the Everlasting Covenant. The story of David from childhood through his reign as king can be found in 1 Samuel 16 through 1 Kings 2. We will begin with the covenant initiated by God, though in this biblical account the word "covenant" is never mentioned. However, all the elements of covenant making are present. In fact, Psalm 89 is titled "God's Covenant with David" in some translations, and verses three and four discuss the covenant directly, "You said, 'I have made a covenant with my chosen one, I have sworn to my servant David: I will establish your descendants forever and build your throne for all generations.'"

Understanding the Story

Through this Covenant of Eternal Rule, the "major promises of the Abrahamic Covenant are confirmed and amplified. . . . It is also a confirmation of the Mosaic Covenant."[2] Each covenant is a progressive revelation of kingship. Abraham was made the father of nations; through Moses, Israel was declared a nation that eventually would become ruled by earthly kings; and now through David it was declared that his lineage would reign forever.

THE BACKGROUND

If we take a step back in biblical time, we discover the period of the Judges, which began with Moses and ended when Saul was chosen by God and anointed king by Samuel. King Saul's reign was forty years.[3] It was near the end of that time that Saul lost favor with God, though he continued to rule. Samuel lamented over this fact and the consequences it might have for Israel. In 1 Samuel 16:1 an empathic God speaks to Samuel and challenges him. "The Lord said to Samuel, "How long will you grieve over Saul? I have rejected him from being king over Israel." God then told Samuel to "fill your horn with oil and set out, I will send you to Jesse the Bethlehemite." Samuel, filled with fear, replied, "How can I go? If Saul hears of it, he will kill me" (1 Samuel 16:2). While these fears were justified, God did not let Samuel use them to avoid what needed to be done. God had a plan, gave specific instructions, and Samuel obeyed the word of the Lord, even if he was reluctant.

DAVID'S CALL

The story of David's call is familiar to many Christians. Samuel went to Bethlehem according to God's instructions. Once there, he called for the people to offer a sacrifice to God and to enter into worship. A man named Jesse and his sons were present (at least most of them). God had communicated to Samuel that one of Jesse's sons would be anointed to be the next king. Samuel looked at the eldest; he may have thought, "Surely, this is the one." Samuel would have been right according to cultural tradition that the eldest would receive the highest honor. God, though, did not abide by tradition and said "No, not him." God reminded Samuel that "the Lord does not see as mortals see: they look on outward appearance, but the Lord looks on the heart" (1 Samuel 16:7).

Samuel brought forward each son present, and every time God said no. When it looked like there were no others, Samuel asked Jesse, "Are all your sons here?" There might have been some reluctance in Jesse's voice when he said, "There is the youngest, but he is keeping the sheep." The youngest was the most expendable. It was not necessary for him to be present because he was needed to do the work out in the field.

The people waited as Jesse sent someone to get David. When he arrived at the place where all the people had gathered, Samuel noticed that he was "small in stature," a term that not only referred to his physical height but also that he was the last in line for any familial inheritance. However, God was not concerned with any of that and said, "Rise and anoint him; for this is the one" (1 Samuel 16:12). Samuel took the horn of oil and anointed him. Immediately, scripture tells us, "The spirit of the Lord came mightily upon David from that day forward" (1 Samuel 16:13). Though never clearly stated, God was, once again, entering into a covenantal relationship. God may have chosen David for "demonstrating his pastoral care over the flock entrusted to him—he had proved himself to be a faithful 'shepherd.'"[4] Once again, God called the least likely one into greatness.

THE COVENANT

As the story of David and his kingship unfolds, we become aware that not only was he an adulterer but also a murderer. Even these atrocious deeds did not cause God to turn away from David and nullify the covenant. Prior to his adultery with Bathsheba and the contrived killing of her husband, Uriah, God revealed more of the covenant with David. This does not imply that David's wrongdoings were acceptable. It rather points to our God who forgives and the second chance God allows us to have. Just as Moses' action of violence was not to be justified, David's sins were not to be forgotten. Yet, the grace of God is that despite human sinfulness God finds a way to redeem and transform.

First, David was anointed king of Judah, and then in 2 Samuel 5 he became king of all of Israel. It is not until 2 Samuel 7:1–17, though, that we find God's covenantal promises. These promises were uttered by the prophet Nathan. God had promised to keep King David safe from all of his enemies, and now David was settled in his house and "the Lord had given him rest from all of his enemies around him"(2 Samuel 7:1).

The kingdom was at a temporary peace and there seemed to be stability. At this point David wanted to do something for God and, without seeking God's advice, told the prophet Nathan that he was going to build a house for the ark of the convenant and thus for God. Nathan left without saying anything but that night, "the Lord intervened by way of Nathan with an everlasting promise, a theological statement about the 'house' of David."[5] This promise finds its roots in God's covenant with Moses and the deliverance of the Israelites from Egypt. God reminded David of this when, in verse 6, God says: "I brought up the people of Israel from Egypt." God promises/covenants with David to create "a house not of stone or cedar, but a royal dynasty that the Lord establishes forever."[6] This royal house is not established solely for David and his descendants, it is for all of the Lord's people.

There are two other covenantal promises in this passage. The first one is found in 2 Samuel 7:9 where God says, "I will make for you a great name, like the name of the great ones of the earth." The second part is found in verse 10 when God says: "And I will appoint a place for my people Israel and will plant them, so that they may live in their own place, and be disturbed no more." These promises and this covenant made to David "would not be brought about because of his goodness but through David, God was bringing about His purposes."[7]

WHAT DOES THE COVENANT SAY ABOUT DAVID?

Someone like David would not be the one most of us would pick to be our next president. He seemed to have no special qualities for leadership. In addition, he had the least standing in the family because he was the youngest and the smallest of Jesse's seven sons.

God, however, reminded Samuel (and reminds us) that God does not see the same way we do. God needed a person who would follow the commandments issued, and who would be a faithful servant. David was that person, but he had some growing up to do. There is a well-known saying that God does not call the equipped but equips the called. David's story demonstrates this. We know that as a boy he slew the giant Goliath and defeated the Philistines when all hope seemed lost. It was from that point forward that he served King Saul.

During these years, David gained skills he would need to be king. Perhaps even more important is the fact that David was trustworthy. He served King Saul faithfully. Over time, Saul developed a raging jealousy of David, which may have been fueled by the knowledge that Samuel had anointed him. When Saul's jealousy became uncontrollable, he ordered David to be murdered, so David went into hiding.

In this drama, there came a moment when David had the opportunity to kill Saul. In 1 Samuel 24, Saul and his men had just returned from fighting the Philistines (again) when he was told that David was in the wilderness in En-gedi. Saul took three thousand men and pursued David. Now, in what I see as God's great sense of humor, we read that, "He [Saul] came to the sheepfolds beside the road, where there was a cave; and Saul went in to relieve himself" (1 Samuel 24:3). David and his men were hiding deep inside that same cave. Now, since Saul was taking care of personal matters he would have entered that cave all alone; an easy target for David. Yet, David restrained his men. He quietly approached Saul and cut a corner off of his cloak and retreated into the darkness. Instantly he felt remorseful for he had done harm to the Lord's current anointed one. This prompted David to come out of the cave and call out to Saul. He said,

> This very day your eyes have seen how the Lord gave you into my hand in the cave; and some urged me to kill you, but I spared you. I said, 'I will not raise my hand against my lord; for he is the Lord's anointed.' See, my father, see the corner of your cloak in my hand; for by the fact that I cut off the corner of your cloak, and did not kill you, you may know for certain that there is no wrong or treason in my hands. I have not sinned against you. (1 Samuel 24: 10–11)

From David's point of view, this action was rooted in his covenant with Jonathan and the spoken agreement to do no harm to any of King Saul's family. As part of the covenantal agreement if David had intentionally injured or killed King Saul or any member of his family, then the covenant would be broken and Jonathan would be free to seek retribution.

This divine covenant with David tells us that from ordinary beginnings God saw extraordinary possibilities in a young shepherd boy. Even if David's future grievous sins disappointed God, because David truly repented, God's grace surrounded him; God did not destroy David. He was still king, and God kept the promise of earthly rule through David's son Solomon.

PROMISES AND CONDITIONS

In the beginning, Adam and Eve were warned not to eat of the tree of knowledge; Abraham was told to walk before God and be blameless; while Moses was given the condition that the people were to obey the law and the commandments. God's covenant with David is like God's covenant with Noah, in that there were no stated conditions that needed to be followed. David was not required to do anything.

However, God did tell David of a condition that was in effect with Solomon. God said:

> I will raise up your offspring after you, who shall come forth from your body, and I will establish his kingdom. He shall build a house for my name, and I will establish the throne of his kingdom forever. I will be a father to him, and he shall be a son to me. When he commits iniquity, I will punish him with a rod such as mortals use, with blows inflicted by human beings. But I will not take my steadfast love from him, as I took it from Saul, whom I put away from before you. (2 Samuel 7:12–15)

The condition was that if Solomon sinned, he would be punished. Yet, God did not state that this condition could erase the promise of eternal rule.

This promise was one of the blessings God gave to David. It would be interrupted when the kingdom became divided, and again when the Northern Kingdom, and subsequently, the Southern Kingdom were taken into captivity by foreign powers. Yet, God did not forget this blessing/promise, nor the covenants with Adam, Noah, Abraham, or Moses. The eternal reign would be instituted in the everlasting covenant with Christ Jesus.

There were other blessings: rest from his enemies, a home to live in, and land for his people. These were at the heart of God's blessings seen throughout the scriptures: God is protector and provider. David's people lived in relatively peaceful times until his death. They had plenty, and they prospered.

COVENANT MAKING

1 Chronicles (and also 2 Samuel 6) has more of David's story for us to explore. Specifically, this is where many scholars believe the covenant meal with David is found.

David assembled all the Israelites and called all the priests, all the descendants of Aaron and Levi. He ordered them to sanctify themselves, so that they were pure, and had them prepare a burnt offering to God. After that was done, they went and carried the ark of the covenant back to Jerusalem.

After the ark was properly placed in the sacred tent, David had the priests, once again, offer burnt offerings and give offerings of well-being in thankfulness for the safe journey and the return of the ark. Following this, David blessed the whole assembly and distributed to every man and woman a loaf of bread, a portion of meat, and a cake of raisins (1 Chronicles 16:1–3).

David had the priests sacrifice rams and other appropriate animals. This was the blood of consecration that signified David acknowledged God as the one who guided him and his army and who protected them and allowed the people to build homes and settle down in Jerusalem. It was following these signs of a blood seal and a covenant meal that God specifically gave the promises and blessings we learned about.

Understanding the Covenant's Relevance

WHAT DOES THIS COVENANT SAY TO US TODAY ABOUT OUR JOURNEY AS DISCIPLES?

It was scarcely three generations after David's reign, before the United Kingdom of Israel divided due to a dispute with Solomon's son, Rehoboam. Both the Southern and Northern Kingdoms eventually fell—the Northern Kingdom fell to the Assyrians in 720 BCE and the Southern Kingdom of Judah fell to the Babylonians in 597 BCE. When most of the Israelites had been conquered, the reign of David effectively ended. "His literal throne exists no more."[8] It must have been a devastating time; and many had to wonder just where God and the promises made to David and Abraham had gone.

God, though, never abandoned the people of Israel that were in Babylon. There they were allowed to live as Jews and to worship their God. In fact in Jeremiah 29, we find that the prophet wrote a letter from God to encourage all in Babylon:

> Thus says the Lord of hosts, the God of Israel, to all the exiles whom I have sent into exile from Jerusalem to Babylon: Build houses and live in them; plant gardens and eat what they produce. Take wives and have sons and daughters; take wives for your sons, and give your daughters in marriage, that they may bear sons and daughters; multiply there, and do not decrease. But seek the welfare of the city where I have sent you into exile, and pray to the Lord on its behalf, for in its welfare you will find your welfare. (Jeremiah 29:4–7)

These words are important because God had promised David eternal rule, a land for his people and peace throughout. While it seemed that God did not keep the covenant; that was not true. God's word is forever; it can never be erased. The Israelites, though, made choices that led to their being conquered. The words of Jeremiah revealed that God was always there, always seeking the welfare of the Israelite people, and would keep the covenantal promises, even though there was quite a detour.

This covenant and the period where God seemed silent is a great story for us as individuals, as a church, and as a community. There probably has been a time in each of our lives when we felt the lack of God's presence. St. John of the Cross, a sixteenth-century Carmelite monk used the phrase "the dark night of the soul" to describe a challenging period of his own life. I am sure that many of the Israelites in captivity would have felt this way. For several centuries, the Hebrew people were invaded numerous times by foreign powers. They experienced one trauma after another—the fall of Samaria, relocation to Assyrian lands, the fall of Jerusalem, exile under the Babylonian rule, and perhaps the worst of all, the destruction of the Temple, the home of God's presence and their spiritual community. As they were forcefully scattered to foreign lands, the Hebrew people would have been so painfully gripped by the sense of loss and despair. God might have seemed so distant.

I know that there have been seasons in my life too when God seemed distant. One such season was when I was in my late twenties. I had just graduated from the University of Arizona with a Master of Science in Nursing degree; and was director of education at Hillhaven Hospice, at that time one of only three hospices in the United States. While I went to church, I was unsure of what I truly believed in, and still felt that God did not care about me. Being a Christian, for me, was simply going through the right motions. Many times I heard of God's promises to those who followed Christ Jesus; promises of forgiveness and of the grace to begin again regardless of our past. I simply did not believe it.

A year earlier, while I was still in school, I attended a Campus Crusade event. As we walked into the room we were given a check with our name on it.

Mine said, "payable to Evy McDonald" and the amount was "unlimited love and forgiveness." It was signed: Jesus Christ. Immediately, I tore that check into tiny pieces, tossed it on the floor, and walked out. It made no sense to me. In my experience God had abandoned me when I had polio at the age of eighteen months.

I was not sure why I was going to a United Methodist church but I did; perhaps it was because of a group of young adults that I enjoyed being with. I had never felt God's presence or love. But all of that changed when I was asked to attend a weekend Lay Witness Mission. I was interested in the man who asked me, so I went to be with him. In that weekend I heard the words Jeremiah wrote to the Israelites in Babylon. They were woven into one woman's story and her story sounded a lot like mine. Because of her witness, my thoughts about God began to change, though it would be a circuitous route until I arrived at the point where I knew God loved me and I was forgiven. In my life journey, I discovered that even when I thought God was absent, God was there all the time; I just had to reach out and seek God.

> Professing Christians often complain that God's promises are not realities in their lives. They claim to know God and say they know the promises are true, but they cannot understand why they do not experience them. This leaves them puzzled. . . . Many think they have fulfilled the requirements when they haven't. Many think they have faith when they don't. The Scriptures give us many assurances that the promises will be accomplished in all who have the obedience, faith, and intense thirsting for God that Abraham and David had.[9]

This covenant with David can bring us reassurance that God is ever-present in our lives regardless of our experience of that truth. God is there, as God was for the Israelites when David was king, and when the kingdom had been destroyed and they were in captivity. God may at times seem distant, but in fact God never abandons us and is always with us.

WHAT DOES THIS COVENANT
SAY ABOUT THE CHURCH AND OUR STRUCTURES?

Many United Methodist pastors and congregations today are asking questions about the relevancy of our brick and mortar church structures, especially if they are in need of extensive repair. Once again, we can look at God's covenant with David for guidance. Structures need to serve a purpose but that purpose is not everlasting; it is not the same as a covenant. David in 2 Samuel 7 lived in a beautiful home, and the sacred ark was housed in a tent of canvas, but, David wanted to build a temple for the ark.

As we learned, it was God through the prophet Nathan who told David that he was not to build a temple; that would come later. The ark had served a purpose in being mobile and not constrained to one place. It was perfectly suited for the Israelites in the wilderness and while they were constantly on the move. Even though they were now settled, David was not allowed to build the temple. We read about this in 1 Chronicles 22.

David had won a war, and was instructed by an angel of the Lord to build an altar and to give a sacrifice for what the Lord had done. David did just that and thought, "Here is where the temple for the ark should be built." David knew, though, that he could not do this, therefore he told his young son Solomon that "the word of the Lord came to me, saying, 'You have shed much blood and have waged great wars; you shall not build a house to my name, because you have shed so much blood in my sight on the earth'" (1 Chronicles 22:8). Arthur Pink noted "that the aspect of the divine character revealed in those events was different from that which worship mainly disclosed; therefore, there had been an evident incongruity in one who had shed so much blood erecting a house for the God of mercy and grace."[10] The intended house of prayer was to be built, but it required that peaceful conditions prevailed. David accepted this judgment; but gathered all the materials so that after his death Solomon could build the temple when the time was appropriate.

What this story tells us is that the church structure needs to be one that is not steeped in conflict; it needs to be a place where those who enter the space feel God's grace and know that this is holy ground. David followed God's directions that he would not be the builder; during his reign the ark would remain in its moveable structure. While Solomon eventually built the temple, it was later destroyed by the Babylonians. The second temple was built after the fall of Babylon and the return of the Hebrew people to their homeland, but tragically it was destroyed too by the Roman Empire in 70 CE. Today, the Old City of Jerusalem is marked by walls of an ancient temple, which many believe are from the one Solomon built. But the original structure is gone. From all of this, we can also learn that our structures of brick and mortar are not containers for God or God's actions. As Robert Klein wrote in a commentary, "Congregations who put too much value on their church buildings may have an 'edifice complex.'"[11] There is a need for the holy to be marked and a place for people to gather, but maybe, once again, it needs to be a movable altar.

Think about the founders of Methodism: John and Charles Wesley. Most of their ministry was not done within a formal structure. A common story about Charles is that he even wrote hymns on a horse as it galloped to the next destination. And many scholars believe that Charles wrote new words to familiar tavern tunes. John preached in fields, taverns, workplaces—wherever people gathered. He spoke in a manner that engaged the people's hearts and minds. Together, they wanted to reach people where they were. For John Wesley his "concern was a 'practical divinity' as he called it—the practice of Christian discipleship."[12] We are to be the mind of Christ and walk as Christ walked. Wesley's focus was on "faith working through love which necessitated a synergy of belief and action."[13] There was little need for another formal church. People met in small groups called classes to learn and hold each other accountable for being Christ in the world.

As Methodists and now United Methodists, we are not to just engage in going to church. Richard K. Avery and Donald S. March, the writers of "We Are the Church," a well-known hymn, powerfully witness that "the church is not a building, the church is not a steeple, the church is not a resting place, but the church is a people."[14] As a people, the church is really not a place to which we go but the dynamic community that actively reaches out in Christ's love to the needy and underprivileged of our society. The Rethink Church campaign of The United Methodist Church has challenged congregations to think and act beyond the four walls of our church buildings:

> Church doesn't just happen when we're sitting in the pew. Church happens when we reach out to those who are hungry, sick, or forgotten. When we stand together for justice and inclusion. And when we open our hearts to those who are struggling. That's putting beliefs into action. That's what it means to RETHINK CHURCH.[15]

The church is more than an inwardly focused therapeutic community where members gather to be comforted and find peace in their hearts. The church becomes active and alive, full of the Spirit, when it is outwardly focused and becomes the hands and feet of Jesus, serving the least in our world.

While it is important for us to gather as a community, *The Book of Discipline* tells us that, "No motif in Wesleyan tradition has been more consistent than the link between Christian doctrine and Christian living."[16] We are to be more concerned with acts of mercy, justice, and piety than with our structures. As a faith community, we are called not only to serve the poor with food, clothing, and shelter, but also to give the tools necessary to live a good life. We are to follow the footsteps of those early Methodists, who under John and Charles Wesley built schools, dispensaries, and infirmaries.

One example of Christ-like missions is the Methodist outreach to Korea in the late nineteenth century. The Christian faith was almost unheard of at that time among Koreans. The first thing the Methodist missionaries did was to share the life-giving message of God's love by establishing hospitals and schools, not build a church building. Notably, Mary F. Scranton, the first woman missionary sent to Korea by the Woman's Foreign Missionary Society established the first school for girls, Ewha School for Girls. Women did get education at home, but up until that time, there was no public educational system for women. Home education was typically available for the upper-class women only. This school provided opportunities to learn for girls and women who previously never had such a privilege. Ewha is now one of the finest higher education institutions in South Korea, and the influence of the Methodist missionaries is very much present today.

Comparing the Covenant of Eternal Rule with the First Four Covenants

All the divine covenants speak to the unfolding of God's grace for all of humanity. Through scripture, we can discover that "within the mysteries of eternity—and allowing for our finite understanding of it—God always intended for a redemptive plan to unfold in a manner that can only truly be described as covenantal."[17] Each covenant incorporates the previous ones, and this covenant is no different. Through Noah, God repopulated the earth; through Abraham, God gave the promise of many descendants who would form a nation that would be the bearers of God to all the earth; and through Moses, God gave the Israelites guidance on how to live as a nation; through David, God promised that there would be an eternal kingdom and that its leadership would come through David's lineage.

WHO IS THE COVENANT HOLDER, AND WAS IT BILATERAL OR UNILATERAL?

As with Noah, this was a unilateral covenant. With Noah God made a promise sealed with the rainbow that was not a contractual agreement; there was nothing Noah had to do for that to remain in effect for eternity. The same is true of David, the promise of land and of eternal rule were not tied to certain actions of David or his successors. Whereas the first covenant with Adam and Eve and the covenants with Abraham and Moses were bilateral because each were given conditions that needed to be met.

THE PROMISES AND CONDITIONS

God provided no conditions attached to the promises God made to David. David did not have to be blameless, as God called Abraham to be. Yet, each covenant had a two-fold promise. For Abraham, it was descendants and land; for David, it could be said to be "dynasty and locality—David's line and Jerusalem's throne."[18] God's major covenant promise to David was that he would establish David's kingship for all generations.

THE BLESSINGS FOR KEEPING THE COVENANT AND THE CURSES (CONSEQUENCES) FOR BREAKING IT

The blessings that David received were an extension of all the previous covenants. Through God's covenant with Adam and Eve, then Noah, Moses, and Abraham, God kept the previous blessings and added to them. This was God's effort to give the people of God all they needed to be faithful followers. God made two major covenant blessings that can be seen as obligations. God set the rainbow in the sky as a reminder that God would never again destroy the earth by a flood. God told David that not only would Solomon be the one to build the temple for the ark of the covenant, but also that he would reign with God's blessings. When Solomon's unfaithfulness seemed to threaten the covenant promise, God remembered his own covenant obligations "for the sake of my servant David, and for the sake of Jerusalem" (1 Kings 11:32). This meant that God would not destroy Solomon or deny him a son because of his actions. This clearly means that there were no curses attached to God's covenant with David; neither human beings nor God could break this covenant.

THE COVENANT MEAL

The covenant meal with David was one of bread, dates, and raisins that was shared with the entire community. In contrast, the covenant meal with Moses was a celebration meal with the leaders of the community and done before God's presence; Abraham's covenant meal is considered to be the blessing of bread and wine that he received from the high priest Melchizedek; while Noah's covenant meal is thought to have happened in front of God after God said, "Every moving thing that lives shall be food for you; and just as I gave you the green plants, I give you everything" (Genesis 9:3). Adam and Eve's covenant meal is considered the fruits and vegetables that God gave them to eat, which they could have as much of as they wanted.

I find it fascinating that each covenant meal met the circumstances of that particular setting. At times the meal was extended to the whole community, while other times it was restricted, not because others were not worthy, but because God was acting in a specific way for a particular reason.

Understanding the Covenant between Jonathan and David

David is the only person in the Bible to have an extensive and documented covenant with another human being: Jonathan, son of King Saul. The covenant is made after David slew Goliath and was introduced to the king. We do not know how the bond between the two of them grew, but it may be that in David's bravery and actions against seemingly insurmountable odds, Jonathan "saw that David was what every son of Israel, every faithful warrior should be."[19] In 1 Samuel 18:1–4 we can read about their covenant. 1 Samuel 19:1–3 is an example of how this covenant was lived out on the part of Jonathan. More about this friendship is revealed in 1 Samuel 20.

As we study this covenant, pay close attention to what David and Jonathan did to seal the covenant; how sacred it was; and what would happen if either one of them broke the covenant. This covenant can be a model for us, and it is similar to how Jesus, as God's son, made a covenant with us. Therefore, there is much we can learn from this Covenant of Everlasting Friendship that will inform not only our relationship with God and Jesus, but also with all Christian disciples.

The Covenant of Everlasting Friendship

Those who are raised in the Jewish tradition understand the sacredness of God's covenants with all of Israel. Since the time of Abraham every Jewish boy had been circumcised eight days after they were born; and they were taught that this action set them apart from all the other tribes or nations. They knew that the rainbow was a significant sign of God's unwavering promises, which was given to Noah after the flood. The elders of their community would have told stories of Isaac, Jacob, the twelve tribes, and their history of following God and turning away from God. Each would have heard of the consequences of attempting to nullify or ignore a covenant God had made with their people. They would have realized that covenant called for commitment not just on the part of a few but on everyone who claimed to be an Israelite.

THE ELEMENTS OF THE COVENANT

David and Jonathan would have been aware of the standard elements of covenant making that were to occur between two people entering into this sacred relationship. There was the exchange of robes, the exchange of belts, the exchange of weapons, an animal sacrifice, the walk of death, a mark on the body that bound the two parties together, the pronouncement of blessings and curses, the covenant meal, and the exchange of names.[20]

In 1 Samuel 18:4 we read about the initial steps Jonathan took to covenant with David. "Jonathan stripped himself of the robe that he was wearing, and gave it to David, he also gave his armor, and even his sword and his bow and his belt." When Jonathan gave David his robe, he was giving him his identity because "ancient peoples believed that an individual's clothes were an outward expression of the man. In essence Jonathan gave of himself to David."[21] This action told David "You are no longer alone. . . . You have put on me!"[22] In legal terms, this meant that David received Jonathan's royal heritage; and from that hour their hearts were as one.[23]

As Jonathan took off his armor and belt and handed both of them to David, he symbolically gave David his strength.[24] This act meant that in any battle Jonathan would be there to protect David. The sword and bow were Jonathan's main weapons of war. When he gave these items to David, they symbolized "an exchange of enemies and declared that as covenant partners they would not only protect each other from harm but also join the battle on their partner's side."[25] For Jonathan this meant that even if his father's army was attacking David, he would defend David and his men. This covenant surpassed any promises given to family. Their covenantal promises went far beyond their earthly lives and extended to all of their descendants.

An integral part of ancient covenant making involved a blood ritual. Blood was considered the life force and was held as sacred. Most often in this ritual, both individuals cut their wrists and held them together, mixing their blood.

The significance of this act was that the two became one; they were united forever. While it is not clear if David and Jonathan did this, some scholars believe that this act simply was not recorded. In 1 Samuel 20, King Saul became very angry with Jonathan when he defended David's absence from the king's table. Saul declared that the son of Jesse, meaning David, was to die.

The next day, Jonathan went to David's hiding place and through a prearranged signal he indicated to David that the king was after him. David came out from his secret shelter and in an act of worship bowed three times. The two wept and Jonathan said: "Go in peace, since both of us have sworn in the name of the Lord, saying, 'The Lord shall be between me and you, and between my descendants and your descendants, forever'" (1 Samuel 20:42). As a result of these exchanges and the closeness of their friendship, it seems clear that they had become blood brothers.[26]

In the introduction, I wrote about doing this same action with my best friend Arty. I also remember when I pricked a finger with Nancy; as we held our fingers together we recited a pledge that stated we were now sisters. Even in my childhood, I understood that these actions created a special bond. It is also thought that a handshake to seal a deal or to make a promise has its origins in this ancient custom. For in a handshake the two wrists would come together and touch at the point others, perhaps like Jonathan and David, would have cut their wrists.

It is important to note that Jonathan was Saul's oldest son. He was the legitimate heir to the throne; but Samuel had already anointed David as the next king. According to cultural customs, therefore, Jonathan and David should have been mortal enemies. Instead, they were covenant partners; and from the day they entered into this relationship they no longer could only think of their personal well-being. A sacred covenant relationship meant you did not make decisions without taking into account how your actions or choices would affect your covenant partner.

This is demonstrated by Jonathan when his father, King Saul, was once again on the hunt for David. Jonathan could have remained silent and just let life enfold without his intervention; thus he would have remained in the good graces of his father. Instead, Jonathan set out and went to David at Horesh. When he arrived, Jonathan told David, "Do not be afraid; for the hand of my father Saul shall not find you; you shall be king over Israel, and I shall be second to you. . . . then the two of them made a covenant before the Lord" (1 Samuel 23:17–18).

THE PROMISES FOR KEEPING THE COVENANT
AND CURSES (CONSEQUENCES) FOR BREAKING IT

David and Jonathan promised to be there for each other, regardless of what King Saul ordered or expected Jonathan to do. If it would violate their covenant neither would follow the king's commands. In 1 Samuel 20, David and Jonathan speak, once again, about Saul's anger toward David. David invokes the covenant with Jonathan when he says: "Therefore deal kindly with your servant, for you have brought your servant into a sacred covenant with you. But if there is guilt in me, kill me yourself; why should you bring me to your father?" (1 Samuel 20:8). David is saying, "If my actions have caused your father to be angry at me or at you, then I have violated our covenant and the penalty should be my death." Jonathan assures David that he has done nothing wrong. He reiterates the consequences for himself of violating the covenant; and gives David encouragement, as a covenant partner should, when he says: "But if my father intends to do you harm, the Lord do so to Jonathan, and more also, if I do not disclose it to you, and send you away, so that you may go in safety. May the Lord be with you, as he has been with my father" (1 Samuel 20:13).

Jonathan, though, needed to hear David affirm a promise of the covenant. He said, "If I am still alive, show me the faithful love of the Lord; but if I die, never cut off your faithful love from my house, even if the Lord were to cut off every one of the enemies of David from the face of the earth" (1 Samuel 20:14–15). David kept this covenantal promise. After Saul and Jonathan's death, he searched out Mephibosheth, Jonathan's son and only surviving relative, who was unable to walk due to being injured at the age of five, when his nurse tried to smuggle him out of danger. David made him an equal member of the ruling family. Mephibosheth, deemed unworthy by society's standards due to his infirmity, was invited to the banquet table.

WHAT DOES THIS COVENANT SAY TO US TODAY?

One of the striking features of this covenant with Jonathan is that it transcended cultural or familial loyalties. As we followed the story of David and all its twists and turns, we discovered that there were two times David could have killed King Saul. He chose an action his men did not understand; but David was clear that Saul was the Lord's anointed one. He was not going to pass judgment on someone called by God. In addition, he was in a covenantal relationship with Jonathan, and that extended to the entire family. David walked away from an opportunity for righteous revenge even though he knew that Saul would have murdered David if he had found the opportunity.

In 1989, protestors filled Tiananmen Square in Beijing in a demonstration for democracy and the right to vote. A CNN news crew captured the video of a young man standing in front of a tank; the driver of the tank refused to run over him, thus this young man's life was saved. While we do not know the whole story, we can conclude that the tank driver did not see this man as a threat, and perhaps he saw him as a "brother." This is covenantal living between human beings in action. When we do not see each other as enemies, there are many more choices we can make in how to deal with differences. I am not simplifying the complex problems of violence in our world today; but can you imagine what difference it could make if we thought in covenantal terms with all of our neighbors; even those we do not agree with or even like?

HOW DOES THIS COVENANT INFORM OUR CHRISTIAN DISCIPLESHIP?

When we say yes to being a disciple and commit our lives to living as Jesus taught us, we are in a covenant relationship with Jesus, other Christian disciples, and with anyone Jesus would have us reach out to. David and Jonathan can be a blueprint for us in how to deal with adversity, hatred, uncertainty, and even fear. Through this covenant we find two individuals who knew that the agreements they had made with each other also included God, therefore they were sacred and infused with God's holiness. Our vows in The United Methodist Church are covenantal vows, and while they do not seem to follow the same formula we find in the First Testament, and here, with David and Jonathan, they are made in Christ's name. We have a covenantal partner in Christ, and our vows include in that alliance anyone in the world, regardless if they made the same vows or not. We are to do as Jesus did and embrace the stranger or alien.

LOOKING AHEAD

King David ruled over the United Kingdom of Israel. After his death there was infighting, and ten of the twelve tribes split off. God's promise of a king forever from the lineage of David was thwarted by humanity's shortsightedness. It was decades and centuries after this split that the next major events took place in the history of the Israelites. Both the Northern and Southern Kingdoms fell to the superpowers of that time, the Assyrians and Babylonians, respectively. Most of the Jews were exiled to foreign lands. Some did remain in the now destroyed city, but these were the ones the Babylonians saw no value in. It is from these people that the prophet Jeremiah rose.

Many Christians believe that the words of Jeremiah 29:11–14a and Jeremiah 31:31–34 are foretellers of the birth of Jesus. In Chapter 29 the prophet writes these words from God, "For surely I know the plans I have for you, says the Lord, plans for your welfare and not for harm, to give you a future with hope. Then when you call upon me and come and pray to me, I will hear you. When you search for me, you will find me; if you seek me with all your heart, I will let you find me says the Lord." And those written in Jeremiah 31:31–34 are:

> The days are surely coming, says the Lord, when I will make a new covenant
> with the house of Israel and the house of Judah. It will not be like the covenant
> that I made with their ancestors when I took them by the hand to bring them

out of the land of Egypt—a covenant that they broke, though I was their husband, says the Lord. But this is the covenant that I will make with the house of Israel after those days, says the Lord: I will put my law within them, and I will write it on their hearts; and I will be their God, and they shall be my people. No longer shall they teach one another, or say to each other, "Know the Lord," for they shall all know me, from the least of them to the greatest, says the Lord; for I will forgive their iniquity, and remember their sin no more.

As we explore the Everlasting Covenant made through Christ Jesus, we will examine the words from Jeremiah and look at how Jesus was a fulfillment of the previous covenants.

Endnotes

1. Arthur W. Pink, *The Divine Covenants* (Memphis: Bottom of the Hill Publishing, 2011), 147.

2. Kevin J. Conner and Ken Malmin, *The Covenants: The Key to God's Relationship with Mankind* (Portland, OR: City Bible Publishing, 1983), 59.

3. Bible Insight, "Biblical Chronology and the Judges of Israel," accessed September 24, 2015, www.bibleinsight.com/judges-chronology.html.

4. Chris Woodall, *Covenant: The Basis of God's Self-Disclosure* (Eugene, OR: Wipf & Stock, 2011), 37.

5. Samuel Giere, "Commentary on 2 Samuel 7:1–11,16," accessed September 24, 2015, www.workingpreacher.org/preaching.aspx?commentary_id=196, 1.

6. Ibid.

7. J. Maurice Wright, *"God's Covenant Plan: Living in Him"* (Maitland, FL: Xulon Press, 2012), 122.

8. Pink, *The Divine Covenants*, 162.

9. Guy Duty, *God's Covenants and Our Time* (Minneapolis: Bethany Fellowship, Inc, 1964), 38.

10. Pink, *The Divine Covenants*, 152.

11. Ralph W. Klein, "Commentary on 2 Samuel 7:1–14a," accessed September 25, 2015, www.workingpreacher.org/preaching.aspx?commentary_id=2528, 1.

12. Richard P. Heitzenrater, *Wesley and the People Called Methodists* (Nashville: Abingdon Press, 1995), 324.

13. Ibid.

14. "We Are the Church," *The United Methodist Hymnal* (Nashville, Abingdon Press, 1989), 558.

15. Rethink Church, home page, accessed April 30, 2016, www.umcom.org/rethink-church.

16. "Our Doctrinal Heritage," *The Book of Discipline of The United Methodist Church*, ¶102 I "Doctrine and Discipline in the Christian Life" (Nashville: Abingdon Press, 2012), 52.

17. Woodall, *Covenant: The Basis of God's Self-Disclosure*, 41.

18. Ibid., 35.

19. Kay Arthur, *Our Covenant God: Living in the Security of His Unfailing Love* (Colorado Springs, CO: WaterBrook Press, 1999), 83.

20. James L. Garlow, *The Covenant: The Study of God's Extraordinary Love for You* (Kansas City: Beacon Hill Press, 1999), 22–25.

21. M. Larry Parino of Rivkah Ministries, "Jonathan and David," accessed September 25, 2015, www.rivkah.org/050818a.htm.

22. Arthur, *Our Covenant God: Living in the Security of His Unfailing Love*, 97.

23. Ibid.

24. Ibid.

25. Garlow, *The Covenant: The Study of God's Extraordinary Love for You*, 22.

26. Parino, "Jonathan and David."

CHAPTER 6

The Everlasting Covenant: The Covenant of Redemption and Grace

Jeremiah's words in Jeremiah 31:31–34 and 29:11 were written to be statements of hope to the Israelites in captivity. He never spoke of an old and new covenant, in the sense that God was going to erase the past covenants. Yes, the Israelites had broken their covenantal agreement with God when many of them began to worship other gods while in Babylon; but God did not walk away from them. Yet, "if it [the covenant] was to come to life again, it must be guaranteed anew by God . . . this means in fact that God pardons and institutes again and anew the old that has been lost. But it is the old, it is not another 'covenant.'"[1] This concept was also echoed by J. Maurice Wright who wrote, "God has never canceled any of His covenants, and consequently they are forever."[2] The words of the prophet Jeremiah tell us this renewed covenant will be written on the hearts of the people and reassures them of God's love and care when it says: "I will be their God and they shall be my people."

Most scholars agree that there were approximately six hundred years between the time of Jeremiah and the birth of Jesus; four hundred of those years are called the silent years; it is the span of time after the last prophet Malachi spoke to the Israelites, and during which there were no more revelations from God through prophets. It is into this hunger for a new word that Mary gave birth to Jesus. In the Book of Matthew, we find that the genealogy of Jesus is traced to David and then to Abraham. This gave Jesus the "legal identity of Christ as the Abrahamic-Davidic Messiah and as the legal heir to David's throne."[3] In a real sense, Israel's covenant God had come to David's house, to the promise of an eternal heir, in person. This was the same God who guided Noah to build an ark, promised Abraham and Sarah that their descendants would be as numerous as the stars, called Moses to be a leader, and promised David that his rule would be forever.

Understanding How Jesus Fulfilled the Covenants

Every time there is a temptation to speak of the old and new covenants as if something had been thrown away, we should recall Jesus' words in Matthew 5:17 where he said, "Do not think that I have come to abolish the law or the prophets; I have not come to abolish but to fulfill."

Understanding this is important to our journey as disciples of Christ. The birth of Jesus was not the beginning of this fulfillment. It began with a God who, from the onset of creation, was determined to be in relationship with human beings. This was a relationship of love, care, grace, and redemption. Just as the prophet Jeremiah was a continuation of this fulfillment when he spoke that God's word would penetrate the heart of the Jewish people, so too was Jesus. The difference is that Jesus became the one human being that had all the laws and the vastness of God's love written on his heart. No other person, on his or her own, has been able to exemplify that. As disciples, when we place the heart of Jesus in our own hearts, then we too will be able to become more and more like him. The teachings of the prophets, the covenants of God, and the life instructions from Jesus will become alive in our words and actions as we seek to emulate Jesus' walk on earth.

HOW DID JESUS FULFILL THE COVENANT OF CARE WITH ADAM?

One understanding of Jesus is that he is the second Adam and that Jesus needed to become human in order to redeem the actions of Adam and Eve. In the covenant God made with Adam, he was called to obey God and to care for all of creation. "God gave Adam a stewardship mandate that has not been rescinded."[4] Adam can be seen to symbolize our inability to do what God asked of him and of us, on our own. As Christians, Jesus gives us a way to renew our part of this covenant with God, to be in a right relationship with God, each other, and all of creation. This is vital to our ability to walk with God as adopted sons and daughters. We do this when we are united with Christ and join with others to not just serve ourselves but serve God's entire world.

Adam had the opportunity, in the fullest sense, to remain in a perfect relationship with God, but that did not happen. God's efforts to lead the people through a series of covenants to become all they were initially intended to be, also did not work as God meant for them to. Even with our inability to follow God's covenants with us, God continued to be in relationship. After four hundred years of silence, God had not left the people. When God chose to establish another covenant, God sent God's self as a human being, called Jesus. Jesus, fully human, obeyed God, even unto death.

Adam and Eve were expelled from the garden, but Jesus was welcomed into the presence of God. Adam and Eve came to know pain and death as part of their lives whereas Jesus overcame death and brought the promise of eternal life with God to fruition through his death and resurrection. The requirements of this covenant remain constant: "God requires a covenant-keeping people," and because of Jesus' faithfulness "meeting this requirement is now made possible by the inner working of the Holy Spirit as opposed to an external command."[5] In Romans 5, Paul reminds us that we are justified by our faith in Christ Jesus, and because of Jesus' sacrifice for us, God's love has been poured into our hearts as foretold by the Prophet Jeremiah. Paul also tells us that just as Adam's actions led to death; Jesus' actions led to an "abundance of grace" (Romans 5:17) and "eternal life" (Romans 5:21).

HOW DID JESUS FULFILL THE COVENANT OF REDEMPTION WITH NOAH?

The covenant God made with Noah was one that allowed human beings to continue to exist, and it was a way for humanity to begin again. Noah and his descendants were redeemed from the consequences of the flood, and their lives were spared. This act of redemption was an act of grace, which came from the heart of God. The grace was bestowed upon Noah and his family initially, but this action extended to all of humanity that came into being after the flood. According to theologian Wayne Grudem this grace is called "common grace" meaning that it is "the grace of God . . . common to all people and is not restricted to believers."[6] United Methodists call this "prevenient grace." Jesus fulfilled this covenant by bringing a saving or justifying grace, which differs from the common grace described by Grudem. The saving grace, which followers of Jesus experience, comes from his death and resurrection.

As with all the divine covenants, the covenant with Noah and the covenant through Jesus were begun with God. Jesus fulfilled the Noahic covenant by being the embodiment of a divine grace that is available to all. This is a distinct difference, in that God's word to never again flood the earth was extended to believers and nonbelievers alike, but humans and in this case including Noah and his family members continued to sin and there was no promise of further redemption. Now, while we do still sin when we turn from what God calls us to do, we have Jesus' life, death, and resurrection to redeem us completely, not just from a flood, but from sin itself.

HOW DID JESUS FULFILL THE COVENANT OF BLESSING WITH ABRAHAM?

God's covenant with Abraham was everlasting, but it had one requirement: that Abraham walk blamelessly before God. This condition would have extended to all of Abraham and Sarah's descendants, just as the blessing of land continued to be a promise to each successive generation. Abraham is known as the father of faith and Jesus is in his line of descendants. Galatians 3:29 reminds those who profess to Christ's followers that "if you belong to Christ, then you are Abraham's offspring, heirs according to the promise." The Apostle Paul is making the point that the "real spiritual descendants of Abraham are not his physical descendants but those of faith. Those who believe that there is one who makes promises and keeps them, are justified by faith as Abraham was."[7] Paul notes that the covenant God made with Abraham was established prior to the requirement of circumcision. This led the way for all people to be part of God's redemptive plan. "Thus, the line of Abraham's inheritance includes all those who are justified by faith, irrespective of gender, race, cultural productivity, social status or any other distinguishing feature."[8]

While God's covenant with Abraham can be seen as a foretaste of God's plan of salvation, the Israelites did not continue to obey God as they had been instructed. Jesus, named in the lineage of Abraham in Matthew's Gospel (Matthew 1:1-17), came in the flesh as both human and divine to reestablish God's promises with the people of God. In Luke's lineage of Jesus (Luke 3:23–38), Jesus' connection to Adam is emphasized. Despite human failures, God was faithful to the covenantal relationship. Jesus fulfilled God's covenant with humanity by calling all who declare themselves to be disciples into union with him and thus with God.

You and I are Abraham's sons and daughters in faith. This did not become annulled with Christ, in fact, our faith derives from Abraham's faith that was passed on from generation to generation and is found in the life, teachings, death, and resurrection of Jesus.

Two stories of Jesus healing women had a profound effect on my faith journey. They can be found in Mark 5 and Luke 13. What they have in common is that Jesus called each woman a daughter, and in the story from Luke, he specifically named her a daughter of Abraham. As a person with a disability, I identified with both of these women, and felt unworthy, as I perceived they did. At the same time, I had longed to experience the sense that I was claimed by Jesus. For many years though, I believed that since I was not physically perfect and considered myself to be damaged goods, I deserved less of God's grace and love.

In these gospel texts, I found a Jesus, and by extension a God, who loved everyone, who reached out to women who seemed to be like me. It made no difference that I still wore a brace; I was able to finally find the emotional and spiritual healing that I sought.

At the time, I had no knowledge of divine covenants or how God acted through human beings to lead God's people forward toward redemption. When I began to understand the significance of these covenants, I realized that my healing, my growth in faith, and my increased commitment to discipleship were a direct result of all the covenants. Without my study of the Bible, I would have never found the deep healing that I needed desperately to believe that God loved me and also that I could love myself and thus love others.

HOW DID JESUS FULFILL THE COVENANT OF LAW AND GUIDANCE MADE WITH MOSES?

God's covenant with Moses is the only one that truly was focused on all the tribes of Israel rather than on an individual, and was given to them as a blueprint for how they were to become a nation. "The Moses covenant proved to be impossible for Israel to keep. The difficulty arose because of the need to obey all of the law, all of the time. This was not possible because of the sin nature within mankind."[9] The Israelites could and did perform animal sacrifices to place themselves back in a right relationship with God. This, though, was a never-ending cycle. God created a dramatic change through Jesus. According to many theologians the life, death, and resurrection of Jesus "ushered in the next phase of God's overall covenant"[10] that was found in the First Testament; this is the Everlasting Covenant, or God's Covenant of Grace.

Writers and theologians Dr. Michael Fitch and Geoff Hawley remind us that, "in some ways this new covenant is even more challenging than the Covenant of Law, but along with it comes additional help. This help comes in the form of the Holy Spirit or Comforter."[11] In being the only human who could fulfill all the laws, Jesus in his compassion told the disciples that God would send the Holy Spirit to guide and strengthen them. Now, God was not going to leave us to our own devices; the way to become the people God created us to be would be not only written on our hearts but, also, through the Holy Spirit, we were given the means to choose good over evil and right over wrong.

When God ushered in the Everlasting Covenant, the law given to Moses did not become irrelevant. On the contrary, Paul in Galatians 5 teaches that the law, especially the Ten Commandments, help to define sin in God's eyes. Now, though, as believers in Christ Jesus, we do not obey the law simply for its own sake, but use it to help guide us as the Holy Spirit leads us to a life that is filled with grace, love, tolerance, and forgiveness.

Just after Jesus taught the Beatitudes, in what we know as the Sermon on the Mount, he said in Matthew 5:18–20:

> For truly I tell you, until heaven and earth pass away, not one letter, not one stroke of a letter, will pass from the law until all is accomplished. Therefore, whoever breaks one of the least of these commandments, and teaches others to do the same, will be called least in the kingdom of heaven; but whoever does them and teaches them will be called great in the kingdom of heaven. For I tell you, unless your righteousness exceeds that of the scribes and Pharisees, you will never enter the kingdom of heaven.

Jesus fulfilled God's covenant with Moses when he taught us the necessity to follow the commandments. Jesus was obedient to God, but it did not mean that he was blindly obedient to the law. Jesus' understanding of the law seemed rather complex. The gospels report that he was not afraid of disobeying the law on several occasions: He often ate with the so-called sinners and he did not always observe the sabbath rules. On the other hand, he also showed a deep respect for the law when he said he had come to fulfill the law (Matthew 5:17). We would receive the blessings of the Beatitudes as we lived out the commandments through the power of the Holy Spirit, the leadership of Jesus, and the forgiving grace of God.

HOW DID JESUS FULFILL THE COVENANT OF ETERNAL RULE GIVEN TO DAVID?

"In many ways, the promise made to David can only be regarded as having been fulfilled in Christ. David had received divine assurance that his monarchial line would endure forever."[12] Some people within the Christian community do not like to equate Jesus with the title "king" due to its allusion to a hierarchical and dominant power. While we admit the limit of this title, we can also say that Jesus is our ruler and king, for he is the fulfillment of the covenant made with David. Furthermore, Jesus is not a king of a physical domain but of the spiritual realm, from which all creation emanates. Perhaps God used the Covenant of Eternal Rule as a way to prepare the minds and hearts of those who follow Jesus to recognize and accept him as the Messiah, as the one who was the heir to the throne of David.

Who is the ruler of our lives as disciples? When I finally gave the reigns of my life over to Jesus and admitted that I was not in control, Jesus, in essence, became the king of my life. By the power of my baptism, I was anointed with the Holy Spirit, which nudges me and attempts to push me down the path God intends for me to walk. Yet, I always have the choice to comply or turn away. The grace that comes with Jesus and the Covenant of Eternal Rule is that I am not left to my own devices to figure out my life. When I stray, there is an accessible pathway back into the arms of Christ.

This truth also applies to our faith communities. As we attempt to live out our calling in our diverse local contexts, we need to realize that we are not in charge. It takes prayer, reflection, scriptural study, discussion, action, more prayer, and more reflection to discern the right next steps. When God is central to this process, we are never alone and together can accomplish far more than we could ever imagine.

In Acts 13, the Apostle Paul and Barnabas spoke to a group of Israelites in Antioch of Pisidia and told them that God spoke of King David when he said, "I have found David, son of Jesse, to be a man after my heart, who will carry out all my wishes" (Acts 13:22). In the following verse, Paul went on to say, "Of this man's posterity God has brought to Israel a Savior, Jesus, as he promised." David's earthly rule ended, but God's covenantal promise did not. While there were many generations between David and Jesus, "David was himself a fulfillment of God's promise of a king and this promise is fulfilled also in Christ . . . and will ultimately be fulfilled again at Christ's return."[13]

In essence, through Jesus and the covenant God made with David and all of the previous covenants, God became our covenant partner—a covenant partner that you and I can call upon and the one who understands our temptations and our feelings. When we claim to be a disciple, Jesus is the light for our path that will lead us to live as the people of God.

Exploring How the Covenant between David and Jonathan Is Reflected in God's Covenant with Us through Jesus

We can see parallels to what Jesus did for us through David and Jonathan's covenant.[14] Jesus would have known this story well, and he understood the sacred importance of a covenant. There are elements of Jonathan and David's covenant ritual that we will see in Jesus' actions for and with us. When Jesus was born, God laid the groundwork for a new covenant with the Israelites, subsequently with all the Gentiles, and with everyone who believed that Jesus was sent by God to bring us to a new level of covenant partnership.

THE EXCHANGE OF ROBES, ARMOR, BELTS, AND WEAPONS

Jonathan gave David his royal robe as well as his armor, bow, and other weapons. These were all symbols that represented Jonathan and his identity in life. When he took off the royal robe and gave it to David he was transferring to David his princely heritage. In receiving what Jonathan was offering, David "put on" Jonathan, and their two lives were forever entwined.

In Philippians 2:5, Paul reminds us to let the same mind be in us that was in Christ Jesus. He explains what Jesus did when he wrote, "who, though he was in the form of God, did not regard equality with God as something to be exploited, but emptied himself, taking the form of a slave, being born in human likeness. And being found in human form, he humbled himself and became obedient to the point of death—even death on a cross" (Philippians 2:6–8). Jesus removed his heavenly cloak—his robe of divinity—and took on our form. He became like us so that we would be given the way to receive his identity so we could recognize ourselves as children of the one God, and therefore heirs to the kingdom. This is just like when David put on Jonathan's robe, he became an adopted heir and was to receive all the rights and privileges associated with that position.

When we are baptized and sealed with the Holy Spirit, we have become one with Jesus and our lives are forever interwoven. All of this was done because of God's great love for us. Through these actions, God likened us to "Himself in expectation and hope, to bring him to make God Himself the portion and strength of his soul."[15] When we give our lives over to God and to Christ, we have taken on a new identity. Our lives are no longer our own; we have committed to following God's will for our lives and to living in the same manner as Jesus did when he walked upon this earth. Paul affirmed this when he wrote to the citizens of Corinth, "So if anyone is in Christ there is a new creation, everything old has passed away; see, everything has become new" (2 Corinthians 5:17). This, Paul tells us, came from God who reconciled God's self through Christ, and as we take on Christ we are also made new in the image and likeness of Christ and become ambassadors for Christ. "Clothed in Christ" is also a metaphor in Paul's writing for becoming more like Christ (Romans 13:14, Galatians 3:27).

When Jesus came to earth it was not just for one family, or only for the Israelites, who were his people; his life, death, and resurrection were for everyone. God, through Jesus, made an Everlasting Covenant that ensures every believer has a God who is with them daily. In Matthew 28:20 when Jesus blessed all who gathered around him (even the ones who doubted) he said, "Remember, I am with you always, to the end of the age." This was a covenantal promise that can never be broken. No matter what we do or how far we stray, Jesus is always with us. Jesus will look for us, seek us out, and lead us back home.

King David gives us an example of how living in covenant with each other looks. Recall the story of Mephibosheth, the son of Jonathan, who David sought out after both Saul and Jonathan were killed. Mephibosheth's nurse took him into hiding as Saul and his men were being slaughtered. As previously noted, an accident had left him unable to walk. David went against all of the cultural mandates when he told Mephibosheth not to fear, that he would exhibit *hesed*—loving-kindness towards him. This was an extravagant display of kindness, not just a simple gift. David gave Mephibosheth a new life.

This is our story with Jesus. Even if we were brought up in the church, we can feel broken, unworthy, afraid, and that can make us run away and hide. In *They Like Jesus But Not the Church*, Dan Kimball identifies six major ideas about the church by those who claim to be "spiritual but not religious." According to this research, emerging generations view the church to be (1) an organized religion with a political agenda, (2) judgmental and negative, (3) dominated by males, (4) homophobic, (5) arrogant in claiming all other religions are wrong, and (6) taking the Bible too literally.[16] These perceptions are mostly from those who do not belong to a church. They are not necessarily fully accurate, but do reflect how the church is seen by new generations. Similarly, David Kinnaman explores why young Christians are leaving the church and finds that the churches have failed to be "safe and hospitable places to express doubts."[17] It is a huge challenge for us today to find ways to help the church to become a truly loving, welcoming, and inclusive community, as Jesus taught us to be.

For about twenty years, beginning when I was sixteen, I felt unworthy to be loved. I hid this deep loathing and outwardly acted as if everything was great, but it caused me to question God and the teachings of the church. Periodically, I would return to organized religion but it never lasted very long. I always had my reasons; but the truth was I was afraid. What if I really was not worthy of love or forgiveness? I went into hiding but God found me and, as I have said, I slowly found my way back to finding meaning in church. In that process, Psalm 139 was a touchstone for me because I lived the words in verses 7–10:

> Where can I go from your spirit?
>> Or where can I flee from your presence?
> If I ascend to heaven, you are there;
>> if I make my bed in Sheol, you are there.
> If I take the wings of the morning
>> and settle at the farthest limits of the sea,
> even there your hand shall lead me,
>> and your right hand shall hold me fast.

God never forgot me. God's promises of steadfast love, forgiveness, and mercy have always been with me, since I stepped forward at the age of thirteen and in all honesty gave my life to Christ at a Billy Graham concert. I know now that from that moment on, even when I turned away and kept saying no to God, I had an advocate, a teacher, a brother, a savior who would search me out and welcome me back.

Bishop Kenneth Carter, Jr., in his book *Near the Cross: A Lenten Journey of Prayer* indicates that even though the church today is in the midst of deep divisions and reconciliation can be painful, Jesus searches us out. He reminds us that when we speak the truth in love we will discover that God is present with us—"incarnate in his Son, Jesus Christ, and dwelling in us through the power of the Holy Spirit."[18]

This is the power of living in covenant with God. David and Jonathan's story shows us the power of living in covenant with each other and honoring that covenant, no matter what the culture around us says we should or should not do. When David found out about Mephibosheth, he sent his servant "Ziba to get Mephibosheth—just as God sends the Holy Spirit to pursue us and bring us to Jesus."[19] God is in hot pursuit of any who have said yes and then have turned away, as well as those who have not yet said yes. When we are ready to stop running, God will be right there to catch us. Jesus is constantly asking, "Who does not know the benefits of my covenant through God with you? Find them and bring them to the banquet table."

Understanding Jesus and the Everlasting Covenant

In the First Testament we see three main components to covenant making:

1. Identifying blessings and curses
2. Binding the covenant in blood
3. Participating in a covenant meal

These steps were accomplished with God, as Jesus coming to us to establish the Everlasting Covenant, which will be in effect until Christ comes again.

Many of us become squeamish at the reality that blood is shed in the act of covenant making or covenant renewal in the Bible. When the Israelites, including Joseph and Mary, went to the Temple and offered the appropriate sacrifice, they acknowledged their relationship with the Holy and the covenants that had been established for them through Noah, Abraham, Moses, and David. A covenant with God was sealed through the offering of an animal. Between human beings this could be the slitting of the wrists and the co-mingling of the blood. Clay Trumball, author of *The Blood Covenants*, says people in ancient times believed that:

> The blood represents life; that the giving of blood represents the giving of life; that the receiving of blood represents the receiving of life; that the inter-commingling of blood represents the inter-commingling of natures; and that a divine-human inter-union through blood is the basis of a divine-human inter-communion in the sharing of the flesh of the sacrificial offering as sacred food.[20]

Because of this, we come to see that the blood Jesus shed signified a total giving of his life for us, and that every time we share in Holy Communion we are receiving Jesus' life-giving energy.

THE SEAL OF THE EVERLASTING COVENANT

In the ancient cultures when blood was ritually blended between two people, the two were then committed to each other no matter what happened. If one of them broke the covenant, it would literally require their life. "This was referred to as a 'walk unto death.'"[21] Jesus' death on the cross can be viewed as the way our covenant was sealed. He gave his life and when we believe in his crucifixion and resurrection, we are at heart taking this walk with Jesus. In Mark 8:34 Jesus spoke to the crowd and to his disciples and said, "If any want to become my followers, let them deny themselves and take up their cross and follow me." In this text the Greek verbs for *deny* and *take up* are in a tense that means something happened at one point in time while the verb for *follow me* is in the present tense, which means it is an ongoing action.[22] Jesus tells us that we must take up the cross daily, and keep following him. It has to become a habit that we engage in everyday, in all of our actions.

Jesus gave his life for us. Theologians and everyday folk like you and me may argue about what this means. Yet in the garden of Gethsemane, Jesus prayed to God and said, "If it is possible, let this cup pass from me; yet not what I want but what you want" (Matthew 26:39). Jesus surrendered his own will: He did not run from those who were coming after him, he faced his enemies and thus gave his life, and on the third day he rose from the dead! Now, because of Jesus' sacrifice, all who believe can be covenant partners with the Creator, Christ, and the Holy Spirit in the Everlasting Covenant.

THE COVENANT MEAL

The last meal that Jesus had with his closest disciples was a covenant meal. It is found in Matthew 26:26–28, Mark 14:22–25, Luke 22:19–30, and 1 Corinthians 11:23–25. The Gospel of Matthew records this account:

> While they were eating, Jesus took a loaf of bread, and after blessing it he broke it, gave it to the disciples, and said, "Take, eat; this is my body." Then he took a cup, and after giving thanks he gave it to them, saying, "Drink from it, all of you; for this is my blood of the covenant, which is poured out for many for the forgiveness of sins."

The bread symbolized Jesus' body, which would be broken and the pouring of the wine symbolized his blood that would be shed. This was probably confusing for the disciples at the time. They might not have fully understood what Jesus meant with such words. Yet, in continuing Jesus' practice of table fellowship after his death and resurrection, the disciples would have recognized the deeper meaning of the Last Supper.

The early form of Communion among Jesus' followers was a full meal for baptized believers that included the bread and the wine in memory of Jesus. It was not until the fourth century, when Christianity was recognized as a sanctioned religion, that Communion transitioned from occurring at services in people's homes to the church building itself. A new ritual emerged in which generations of Christians have participated; the meal was no longer a feast. Yet even today, every time we gather at the Communion table and take of the bread and the juice of the vine, we confess our unity and our covenant relationship with Christ and with each other. Our Communion table is the altar of the covenant.

THE CONDITIONS OF THE EVERLASTING COVENANT

Though this covenant is irrevocable, it is not unconditional. God does expect certain things from us. In Matthew 3:1–18 we are told through the story of John the Baptist that we are called to repent, turn away from sin, and receive a new beginning that we now know comes to us through Christ Jesus with the power of the Holy Spirit. While this is the initial condition, it requires ongoing faith. Faith is seen in our worship, in our actions, and in how we treat those who are at the margins of our society. Along with faith comes the requirement of obedience. All three are ongoing actions. Every time we sin, we must repent and with repentance comes a renewed commitment to faithful and obedient living until the teachings of Jesus are etched in our hearts and become the internal standard by which we live.

THE BLESSINGS OF THE EVERLASTING COVENANT

We receive a plethora of blessings when we accept Jesus as our Savior and enter into a covenantal relationship with the triune God. Jesus promises that the Holy Spirit will come to us when we are baptized, and remain with us during our lifetime. We see the beginnings of this in the Book of Acts when both Jews and Gentiles received the power of the Spirit (Acts 2:10–11). Throughout Jesus' ministry, with the disciples after his death and resurrection, and during the early church continuing to today, we can see examples of the gifts of healing, the gift of miracles, and the power to resist sin and temptation. With the resurrection comes the blessing of being with God in this life and the next one.

A Glimpse into Covenantal Living in Two Different Faith Communities

The concept of covenantal living transcends religion, race, and geography. Often, it is beneficial to explore how others understand the bonds that bind a people together as a community that cares for one another. As you read the following, please keep in mind that these two perspectives come from individuals and they are not representative of an entire group.

ONE JEWISH PERSPECTIVE

I sat down with Harpo Jaeger of the National Havurah Committee and talked with him about his perspective on covenants. The National Havurah Committee is a diverse network "dedicated to Jewish living and learning, community building, and *tikkun olam* (repairing the world)."[23] Jaeger grew up in the Havurah movement and it is how he understands his religion. As he attended their retreats he began to feel his faith in a personal way. He not only distinguished himself as Jewish through religious practices but also by wearing a *kippah*, or head covering. This became a way of life for him that identifies him as part of a community. A word used by Jaeger was "obligated."[24] As I listened to him talk about his religious obligations to himself and his community, I recognized he was speaking about a covenantal relationship. He belongs to a small synagogue that reminds him of the Havurah Jewish movement where there is equalitarianism between men and women. In addition, it is a community that comes together, prays together, and experiences the life cycle together.

Jaeger belongs to the millennial generation and he says that the idea of a covenant is not popular. "We live in a liberal worldview where individual choices and autonomy are valued." He explained that entering into a covenant does not come from an authority figure but is a personal decision. It has to do with family and the notion of obligation. He explained that the forefathers had a saying, "You are not obligated to complete a task but nor are you free to neglect it."[25] It is a responsibility that you may not be able to finish, but you do not get to walk away from it. You are in a bonded relationship with others.

When we talked about the covenants that God made with Moses and Abraham. Jaeger said, "Abraham is so central that you don't have to think about him."[26] He could relate to Moses because Moses was responsible for bringing a tribe into religion. From Moses came core values to be followed as a community. One statement from the website for the National Havurah Committee says "the Torah cannot be acquired except in fellowship."[27] For me, this statement underscores why we as communities of faith need to gather, whether we are Christian or Jewish. It is together that we learn of our faith and how to live out our faith in the world so that we bring justice and mercy into our neighborhoods, cities, states, and countries.

ONE NATIVE AMERICAN PERSPECTIVE

The Seven Sacred Principles of the Lakota people are ways to honor and respect the Lakota and other native cultures.[28] I find a correlation to the Ten Commandments that Moses brought down from the mountaintop to the Israelites and thus for the generations that followed. Both are guidelines that relate to the relationship with God or Creator and with each other and all of creation.

Living these principles can only occur through a covenantal relationship with others; a holy promise to follow them and engage in the rituals which, according to the Lakota tradition, will lead to a life of "total health and happiness."[29] Woven within these Sacred Principles are practices and perspectives for the individual and for the community. I will share several, but not all of these principles.

The Second Principle is *Wo-canto' kna-ke*, which is "to have a heartfelt love and compassion for those who are close to you . . . as well as for anyone . . . who may be suffering or who may be praying for help and guidance, whether you have an established relationship with them or not."[30] This is a call for the individual and the community to be compassionate, generous, and forgiving. This practice draws one into a sacred silence, much like the Christian centering prayer, and from there, a compassion for others will naturally emerge.

The Third Sacred Principle, *Wo-wa unsi-la*, is an extension of the second. One's love and compassion extends not only to the human species, but to all of Grandfather's Creation. A deep care for all living things begins to emerge, along with the desire to help any part of creation that is suffering.

The Fourth Sacred Principle, *Wo-wa-wo-ki-ye*, takes the feeling of compassion into action. This is a justice component where one not only thinks about those who are suffering but also does not pass them by. One empathizes with others and connects with others to look around and see what needs to be done. There is a sense of connecting with all of creation. "The language of Lakota spirituality often dovetails with the language of modern quantum physics. The words for the creative life force, Tunkasila or Wakan Tanka literally mean 'lines of energy that run through all things.'"[31]

Connected with this principle are two other truths. In the Lakota community it is important to ask for help from the spirit world and then to be thankful when it is received. This is again similar to the way we pray as Christians. There is a Lakota belief that forgetting to be thankful and to focus on what you lack will stop the flow of abundance. In addition, if one does not give to others, the flow will also be stopped. A central truth is that "we are part of the whole of creation."

These Sacred Principles and the others are to be followed at all times. Like the Ten Commandments, the Lakota people and all who follow these Seven Sacred Principles receive spiritual nourishment that leads to health and happiness. They also are a reference point for how to live in community. As I read these principles, I understand them as a covenant that brings the individual to a closer relationship with the Great Spirit, and with all others who are on this path. Our covenantal relationship with Christ strengthens our connection with all God's people.

Understanding How Living in a Covenantal Relationship with Jesus Affects Our Lives

We are brought into a covenantal relationship with Christ and all believers at our baptism, and we are able to reaffirm this relationship every time we come to the Communion table. Both of these sacraments are directly connected with the inward grace that we receive from our triune God. Baptism gives us new life in Christ and fills us with the power of the Holy Spirit. Communion connects us with all who have partaken (past and present), and all who will partake, in this holy meal. In addition, every time we come to the Communion table we are offered a way to receive forgiveness and mercy. These two ordinances form the foundation of our Christian discipleship.

OUR CHRISTIAN DISCIPLESHIP

When we pledge our lives to God, we are in a covenant relationship that should affect all aspects of our life. No longer are petty jealousies or envy acceptable. When we, with all our heart, want this relationship it demands that we live it daily. No longer are we to be satisfied with saying, "Well, that is just the way I am." God expects more of us because we are given so much. Through our relationship with God, we have access to a power that helps us resist temptation, heals us from our hurts, and shows us a way out of difficult circumstances. Jesus is our faithful friend who will always be there to guide us and remind us that God has named and claimed us.

We, though, do need to make some commitments. This relationship is not just a one-way street where we can sit back, relax, and let God drive the car. It requires action on our part. Our lives can only be in line with God's will if we take time to be with God in prayer, study, conversation, and even in debate. Even if we do all of this, it is still not enough. God calls us to action. Each one of us has to discover the methods and the means by which we are to live out our covenant relationship: how we are to serve; in what ways we need to grow spiritually, emotionally, mentally; and how are we to live in community.

LIFE AS A COMMUNITY OF DISCIPLES

Christ calls us into relational discipleship. This is not a journey we can do by ourselves. It is one where together we have so much more than any one of us has alone. In Mark 6, Jesus sent the disciples out two by two and in Luke 10, Jesus chose seventy other disciples and, once again, sent them out two by two. Nowhere did Jesus tell his disciples that they were to go out on their own. When they returned, he gathered them together to give thanks, share their stories, and to become refreshed from their journeys. This is the church. This is discipleship.

For John Wesley to be a follower of Christ "in a way that renews both individuals and communities required disciplined practices. . . . These disciplined practices gave power and strength to people of the early Methodist movement to live as faithful disciples of Jesus Christ."[32] The participants in the United Society were expected to show their desire to grow in faith by "doing no harm," "doing good," and "attending upon all the ordinances of God."[33] In an effort to make these traditional instructions more easily understood, Bishop Rueben P. Job reintroduced them to contemporary Christians as the three simple rules.[34] Jeanne Torrence Finlay, author of *Three Simple Rules for Christian Living* reminds us that these rules are interrelated. "They are Christian practices that heal the wounds of the world and work for justice. . . . The first two rules, 'do no harm,' and 'do good,' are ways of keeping the commandments to love God and neighbor."[35]

The third rule, stay in love with God, or attend upon all the ordinances of God, gives spiritual disciplines to empower us to live out the first two rules. John Wesley had practices that would enable both individuals and faith communities to stay in love with God. They were: prayer, attending worship, receiving the Lord's Supper, Bible reading and study, and fasting for one day a week from food but not water.[36] If we covenanted as faith communities to follow these rules, then it seems that we would develop an intense desire to share God's goodness, grace, and abundance with the world.

Our faith communities are the body of Christ and the family of God. Yet, we do not always act like people coming together to live out our covenantal relationship with God and Christ. Far too often we stress the individual's needs or desires over what is best for the greater community. The reality is that in many of our congregations we have quarrels over leadership; arguments about what is morally right and what is not; fights over music and the style of worship. I know of churches where people get mad and walk out over these kind of disagreements, and some even left the church. Bishop Kenneth Carter reminds us that "Like relationships between individuals, community also requires sacrifice."[37] He points out that a covenantal or sacrificial community will come together to accomplish something significant. This call will necessitate the whole community to become comfortable with "motion, being called from stability and stasis (even from stuckness!) to the pursuit of a closer and deeper relationship with Jesus Christ. . . . Living and vital churches are always in a state of change."[38]

In Walter Brueggemann's book *The Covenanted Self*, he gives us insights into the teachings of the Apostle Paul. He writes:

> It is an ecclesial issue that prompts Paul when he makes an argument that the church, baptized as we are, is not to conduct its business or settle its disputes like any other community. We are bound to a God for whom the neighbor comes first. So Paul names the categories of life in the church: encouragement in Christ, consolation from love, sharing in the spirit, compassion, sympathy. These five ingredients are the fundamental markings of a community.[39]

Our covenantal relationship with God becomes the touchstone by which we learn how to think as Jesus did, act in accordance with his teachings, and think of the good of the whole over our individual desires. Jesus demonstrates this for us throughout the Gospels; but we can see it clearly in Luke 4.

It is here that Jesus reads from the Prophet Isaiah and declares to his hometown of Nazareth that this scripture was fulfilled in their hearing. What did Jesus say he, and therefore we, were to do? We are to bring good news to the poor, proclaim release to the captives, and let the oppressed go free. John Howard Yoder understands that this proclamation from Isaiah served as the "platform" on which Jesus built his mission.[40] It was like Jesus' mission statement.

Paul writes about being of one mind with Jesus in Philippians 2:1–4 where he admonishes the members of the church in Philippi and us today:

> If then there is any encouragement in Christ, any consolation from love, any sharing in the Spirit, any compassion and sympathy, make my joy complete: be of the same mind, having the same love, being in full accord and of one mind. Do nothing from selfish ambition or conceit, but in humility regard others as better than yourselves. Let each of you look not to your own interests, but to the interests of others. Let the same mind be in you that was in Christ Jesus.

These words need to guide us in living out our covenantal agreement with Christ, which we entered into when we said yes to discipleship. As we grow in our desire and ability to come together, not only as people who worship in a building, but also as those who seek to live with each other and the greater community as guided by Jesus through these words of Paul, we will become more faithful people. He says it all.

The church is the continuation of Jesus' ministry. We serve Jesus, as we reach out to the least in our society, as Jesus indicated in Matthew 25:35–36:

> I was hungry and you gave me food,
> I was thirsty and you gave me something to drink,
> I was a stranger and you welcomed me,
> I was naked and you gave me clothing,
> I was sick and you took care of me,
> I was in prison and you visited me.

In our serving one another, we are making our communities more humane and compassionate places to be.

What would happen if being in covenant truly led us to open our hearts, our minds, and our doors because we did not look to our own interests but to the interests of others? What if we truly believed that God was able to accomplish abundantly far more than all we can ask or imagine (Ephesians 3:20), because we believed in the power of our covenantal relationship? How would that change your faith community?

Conclusion

Covenants are holy and sacred. In this study, we have explored God's covenants with humanity. The stories of Adam and Eve, Noah, Abraham, Moses, David, and their communities help us understand the depth of God's love and justice for all. The covenant through Jesus encompasses all of God's covenants and is foundational to our faith in God.

Different faith traditions will have their own language to express what it means to live together. In the two traditions presented earlier, I found a commonality in caring for others, inside and outside the stated tradition. For those of us who are Christian, as we live out the covenants studied in this book, we will discover that through all of creation flows the generosity of God, and that there is enough for all to live abundantly because our God is limitless and self-giving.

We will find that this God is not exclusive and the same principles can be seen in other faiths. German theologian Jürgen Moltmann in his book *The Coming of God* compares two main Christian understandings of salvation: a double outcome judgment and a universal salvation. The double outcome theology basically claims that, at the last judgment, the believers enjoy the eternal bliss in heaven, while the unbelievers are thrown into the torments of hell. The theology of universal salvation tells us that all are saved, because grace is stronger than any human limitedness. While avoiding a simple dichotomy of these two positions, Moltman powerfully asserts that there is hope for all, because in the end all will be liberated and saved.[41] God's inclusive vision for all defies any human attempts to draw boundaries between the righteous and the wicked, the insiders and outsider, and us and them.

In our Judeo-Christian heritage, God chose to call us into relationship time and again; chose to redeem us and sent Jesus to give us a living example of how to be in relationship with each other, with the stranger, with the marginalized, and with ourselves. Through covenantal relationships we can truly learn how to love God with all our heart, all our mind, and all our strength so that we can accept God's love for us, and thus love our neighbor as ourselves as God asks of us. Blessings on your journey.

Endnotes

1. Norbert Lohfink, *The Covenant Never Revoked: Biblical Reflections on Christian-Jewish Dialogue* (Paulist Press, NY, 1991), 48.

2. J. Maurice Wright, *God's Covenant Plan: Living in Him* (Maitland, FL: Xulon Press, 2012), 100.

3. Guy Duty, *God's Covenants and Our Time* (Minneapolis: Bethany Fellowship, Inc., 1964), 41.

4. Chris Woodall, *Covenant: The Basis of God's Self-Disclosure* (Eugene, OR: Wipf & Stock, 2011), 43.

5. Ibid., 45.

6. Wayne A. Grudem, *Systematic Theology* (Leichester, UK: InterVarsity Press, 1991), 657–58.

7. Wright, *God's Covenant Plan: Living in Him*, 175.

8. Woodall, *Covenant: The Basis of God's Self-Disclosure*, 57.

9. Dr. Michael Fitch and Jeff Hawley, *Covenants, Creation and Choice: Where Theology and Science Overlap* (Bloomington, Indiana: Westbow Press, 2013), 73.

10. Ibid.

11. Ibid.

12. Woodall, *Covenant: The Basis of God's Self-Disclosure*, 72.

13. Rolf Rendtorff, *God's History: A Way Through the Old Testament* (Philadelphia: Westminster, 1969), 67.

14. Kay Arthur, *Our Covenant God: Living in the Security of His Unfailing Love* (Colorado Springs, CO: WaterBrook Press, 2014), 107.

15. Andrew Murray, *The Two Covenants* (Fort Washington, PA: 2013 reprint of 1898 edition), 5.

16. Dan Campbell, *They Like Jesus But Not the Church: Insights From Emerging Generations* (Grand Rapids, MI: Zondervan, 2007), 2.

17. David Kinnaman, *You Lost Me: Why Young Christians Are Leaving Church and Rethinking Faith* (Grand Rapids, MI: Baker Books, 2011), 11.

18. Kenneth H. Carter, Jr., *Near the Cross: A Lenten Journey of Prayer* (Nashville: Abingdon Press, 2015), 79.

19. James Garlow, *The Covenant: A Study of God's Extraordinary Love for You* (Kansas City: Beacon Hill Press,1999), 41.

20. H. Clay Trumbull, *The Blood Covenants* (Kirkwood, MO: Impact Christian Books, 1975 reprint of 1885 edition), 209.

21. Arthur, *Our Covenant God: Living in the Security of His Unfailing Love*, 61.

22. Ibid., 63.

23. The National Havurah Committee, accessed February 17, 2016, http://havurah.org/institute/the-nhc.

24. Harpo Jaeger, treasurer, National Havura Committee, interview with author, January 27, 2016.

25. Ibid.

26. Ibid.

27. The National Havurah Committee, http://havurah.org/institute/the-nhc.

28. The ideas presented in this section come from the teachings of Gilbert Walking Bull, a Lakota elder, presented in the paper, "The Seven Sacred Principles of the Lakota People," written by Cara Burrow at the Tatanka Mani Camp in Hot Springs, South Dakota, with the permission of Gilbert Walking Bull. Gilbert Walking Bull received these teachings from his ancestors, who received them when Lakota culture first began. He lived these principles, and was able to impart them to others. I have permission to present this material from one of the camp directors: Marilynn Bradley. Gilbert Walking Bull has passed on to the Spirit World.

29. Cara Burrow, "The Seven Sacred Principles of the Lakota People" (unpublished paper for Prescott College, 2005), 1.

30. Ibid, 2.

31. Ibid, 3.

32. Jeanne Torrence Finlay, *Three Simple Rules for Christian Living* (Nashville: Abingdon Press, 2008), 5.

33. "Our Doctrinal Heritage," *The Book of Discipline of The United Methodist Church*, ¶102 I "Doctrine and Discipline in the Christian Life" (Nashville: Abingdon Press, 2012), 52.

34. Rueben P. Job, *Three Simple Rules: A Wesleyan Way of Living* (Nashville: Abingdon, 2007).

35. Finlay, *Three Simple Rules for Christian Living*, 5

36. Ibid., 51–54.

37. Carter, *Near the Cross: A Lenten Journey of Prayer*, 56.

38. Ibid., 65.

39. Walter Brueggmann, *The Covenanted Self: Explorations in Law and Covenant* (Fortress Press, Minneapolis, 1999), 85.

40. John Howard Yoder, *The Politics of Jesus* (Grand Rapids, MI: William B. Eerdmans Publishing Company, 1972), 28–29.

41. Jürgen Moltmann, *The Coming of God: Christian Eschatology* (Minneapolis: Fortress Press, 1996), 235–55.

🔖 Epilogue

God has been our covenant maker and covenant keeper from the beginning of creation. As Christians, sometimes we wonder why we need to study the First Testament when we have Christ. We need it because it shows the promises of God from Adam and Eve through David, it leads us to understand how God rescued God's people again and again, and it demonstrates how each covenant builds on all the others, including the Everlasting Covenant through Christ found in the Second Testament.

The earliest followers of Christ only had the First Testament and the oral teachings of Jesus that were passed down. The first communities knew that both sets of instructions were needed because together they show us how God has worked and continues to work in the lives of people. Through the divine covenants, we discover more about who God is and how God reveals God's self. We find a God that remains faithful even when we, both individually and as a people, turn away. Covenant by covenant, we learned of God's forgiveness and God's willingness to not only embrace us again, but lead us out of the morass we put ourselves in. The First Testament gives us glimpses of the God that Jesus called "Abba."

May you discover for yourself the saving grace of God that continues to be at work in your life and in the life of your community. All of these covenants together lead us into a deeper understanding of God's Word and how to apply it to our lives today.

Let us end with a contemporary version of John Wesley's (founder of Methodism) Covenant Prayer:[1]

> I am no longer my own, but yours.
> Put me to what you will, place me with whom you will.

Put me to doing, put me to suffering.

Let me be put to work for you or set aside for you,

Praised for you or criticized for you.

Let me be full, let me be empty.

Let me have all things, let me have nothing.

I freely and fully surrender all things to your glory and service.

And now, O wonderful and holy God,

Creator, Redeemer, and Sustainer,

you are mine, and I am yours.

So be it.

And the covenant which I have made on earth,

Let it also be ratified in heaven. Amen.

Endnotes

1. Jeff Clinger, "Starting a New Worship Service—Looking for Conversation," June 12, 2012, blog, *Changing to Bring Change*, https://changingtobringchange.wordpress.com.

Selected Bibliography

Allen, W. M. Lloyd. "Genesis 9:8–17: A Theological Perspective," year B, vol. 2 in *Feasting on the Word: Preaching the Revised Common Lectionary*." Edited by David L. Bartlett and Barbara Brown Taylor. Louisville, Kentucky: Westminster John Knox Press, 2008.

Arthur, Kay. *Our Covenant God: Living in the Security of His Unfailing Love.* Colorado Spring, Colorado: WaterBrook Press, 2014.

Arthur, Kay and Janna Arndt. *Cracking the Covenant Code.* Eugene, Oregon: Harvest House Publishers, 2012.

Baker-Fletcher, Karen. *Dancing with God: The Trinity From a Womanist Perspective.* St. Louis, Missouri: Chalice Press, 2006.

Barton, John and Julia Bowden. *The Original Story: God, Israel, and the World.* Grand Rapids, Michigan: William B. Eerdmans Publishing Company, 2005.

Bergant, Dianne, CSA. *People of the Covenant: An Invitation to the Old Testament.* Franklin, Wisconsin: Sheed & Ward, 2001.

Brueggemann, Walter. *The Covenanted Self: Explorations in Law and Covenant.* Edited by Patrick D. Miller. Minneapolis: Fortress Press, 1999.

Buber, Martin. *Moses: The Revelation and the Covenant.* New York: Harper & Brothers, 1958.

Burrow, Carol, "The Seven Sacred Principles of the Lakota People." Unpublished paper for Prescott College, 2005.

Campbell, Dan. *They Like Jesus But Not the Church: Insights From Emerging Generations.* Grand Rapids, Michigan: Zondervan, 2007.

Carter, Jr., Kenneth H. *Near the Cross: A Lenten Journey of Prayer*, Nashville: Abingdon Press, 2015.

Debevoise, Daniel M. "Genesis 15:1–12, 17–18: A Theological Perspective," year C, vol. 2 in *Feasting on the Word: Preaching the Revised Common Lectionary.*" Edited by David L. Bartlett and Barbara Brown Taylor. Louisville, Kentucky: Westminster John Knox Press, 2008.

Deiss, Lucien. *God's Word and God's People*. Translated by Matthew J. O'Connell. Collegeville, Minnesota: The Liturgical Press, 1974.

Ferguson, Jane Ann. "Genesis 9:8–17: A Pastoral Perspective," year B vol. 2 in *Feasting on the Word: Preaching the Revised Common Lectionary.*" Edited by David L. Bartlett and Barbara Brown Taylor. Louisville, Kentucky: Westminster John Knox Press, 2008.

Finley, Jeanne Torrence. *Three Simple Rules for Christian Living*, Nashville: Abingdon Press, 2008.

Fretheim, Terence E. "The Book of Genesis: Introduction, Commentary and Reflections," vol. 1 in *The New Interpreter's Bible*. Edited by Leander E. Kech. Nashville: Abingdon Press, 1994.

Gilbert, Kenyatta R. "Genesis 15:1–12, 17–18: A Homiletical Perspective," year C, vol. 2 in *Feasting on the Word: Preaching the Revised Common Lectionary.*" Edited by David L. Bartlett and Barbara Brown Taylor. Louisville, Kentucky: Westminster John Knox Press, 2008.

Grudem, Wayne A. *Systematic Theology.* Leichester, UK: InterVarsity Press, 1991.

Johnson, Elizabeth A. *Quest for the Living God: Mapping Frontiers in the Theology of God*. New York: Bloomsbury Academic, 2007.

Kinnaman, David. *You Lost Me: Why Young Christians Are Leaving Church and Rethinking Faith*. Grand Rapids, Michigan: Baker Books, 2011.

Lee, Jung Young. *The Trinity in Asian Perspective*. Nashville: Abingdon Press, 1997.

Lohfink, Norbert. *The Covenant Never Revoked: Biblical Reflections on Christian-Jewish Dialogue*. New York: Paulist Press, 1991.

McFague, Sallie. *A New Climate for Theology: God, the World, and Global Warming*. Minneapolis: Fortress Press, 2008.

Moltmann, Jürgen. *The Coming of God: Christian Eschatology*. Minneapolis: Fortress Press, 1996.

Murray, Andrew. *The Two Covenants*. Fort Washington, Pennsylvania: 2013 reprint of 1898 edition.

Rendtorff, Rolf. *God's History: A Way Through the Old Testament*. Philadelphia: Westminster, 1969.

Rydelink, Michael. *The Unbreakable Promise: God's Covenants with Abraham, Moses, and David*. Grand Rapids, Michigan: Discovery House Publishers, 2011.

Smick, Elmer. "Covenant," vol. 1 in *Theological Workbook of the Old Testament*. Edited by R. Laird Harris, Gleason L. Archer, and Bruce Waltke. Chicago: Moody Press, 1980.

Stroup, George W. "Exodus 20:1–17: A Theological Perspective," year B, vol. 2 in *Feasting on the Word: Preaching the Revised Common Lectionary*." Edited by David L. Bartlett and Barbara Brown Taylor. Louisville, Kentucky: Westminster John Knox Press, 2008.

Vine, W. E. *Expository Dictionary of New Testament Words*. London: Oliphants, Ltd., 1948.

Whaling, Frank, ed. *John and Charles Wesley: Selected Writings and Hymns*. Mahwah, New Jersey: Paulist Press, 1981.

Woodall, Chris. *Covenant: The Basis of God's Self-Disclosure*. Eugene, Oregon: Wipf & Stock, 2011.

Merriam-Webster's Collegiate Dictionary, 11th edition. Springfield, Massachusetts: Merriam-Webster, 2003.

Yoder, John Howard. *The Politics of Jesus*. Grand Rapids, Michigan: William B. Eerdmans Publishing Company, 1972.

About the Author

Evelyn (Evy) R. McDonald, is an ordained elder in The United Methodist Church and has served rural and inner-city churches. Throughout her life, she has been passionate about caring for and serving with those who live at the margins of society. Prior to becoming a minister, she was a registered nurse and earned a Master of Science in Nursing degree from the University of Arizona. One of her positions was as director of education at Hillhaven Hospice in Tucson, Arizona. At the time, there were only three hospices in the United States, funded by the National Institute of Mental Health as an experiment. She earned her Master in Divinity degree from Union Theological Seminary in New York City and a Doctorate of Ministry degree from Drew University in Madison, New Jersey.

A life-changing detail for her is that as a small toddler she became ill with polio and therefore grew up with a physical disability. In her teens and early adult years, she felt that the church was not welcoming of her and her gifts because of her disability. This began a path towards discovering how we are to live in a faith community with all those we consider "not like us." She currently lives in Tucson, Arizona, where she is writing, teaching, and living with the onset of post-polio syndrome. Her favorite phrase is that no matter what, "God is good, all the time." A quote that has meant a lot to her is:

> When you come to the end of all the light you know, and it's time to step into the darkness of the unknown, faith is knowing that one of two things will happen: Either you will be given something solid to stand on or you will be taught how to fly.
>
> —Edward Teller

Living as a Covenant Community

PARTICIPANT'S GUIDE

elmira Nazombe

🔒 Table of Contents

🐑 Introduction

"Our covenant agreement with God can be summarized as learning to love God with all of our heart, all of our soul, all of our mind, and all of our strength." (*Living as a Covenant Community*, Introduction).

"Together these covenants . . . Tell the story of how God cares for us, acts with and through us, and will continue to unveil ways to live as God's people." (*Living as a Covenant Community*, Chapter 4).

This spiritual growth study offers to each of us an opportunity to pause and take time to look deeply at who God is and at our experiences living as a people of God. The covenants demonstrate aspects of God's unfailing loving-kindness and create and sustain God's relationship with humanity. We will learn about God, but we will also be learning about ourselves. A covenant community is complex and characterized by faith, trust, doubt, obedience—even backsliding—and always struggling to be the covenant partner that God intended, especially in times of crisis.

This study will be an opportunity to think about God's covenant activity in three ways:

- God as the covenant maker, who initiates out of love a relationship with humanity.
- God as the covenant keeper, who never turns away from the covenant people no matter how often they stray from faithfulness.
- God as the covenant equipper, who provides the guidance that the covenant community needs in order to live as God's people and take responsibility for the whole of God's creation and just relationships with their neighbors.

We will have an opportunity to see ourselves in the lives of Adam and Eve, Noah, Abraham, Moses, David, and Jonathan as they act and receive the covenants of Grace, Redemption and Safety, Blessing, Guidance and Law, Eternal Rule, and finally the Everlasting Covenant. As Christians, we will come to understand that we are the covenant community, inheritors of the promises made by God to the covenant communities of the First Testament, commonly called the Old Testament. We will see how Jesus represents the fulfillment of the covenants and God's everlasting promise. We will see how we can be a part of this covenant if we are willing to answer the call to be the covenant community that takes responsibility for the whole of creation and for the life of justice that God intended.

When we enter into a spiritual growth study such as this, we must commit ourselves to being serious about our learning process. We may be doing this study with others, or we may be working on our own. In either case, we need to follow John Wesley's guidance for learning: Bible study—prayerful listening again to the Biblical texts, understanding the traditions of the church, using our own reasoning, and taking into account present realities in the light of our own experience. We will need all of these as we embark upon the task of understanding the covenants and their meaning for our lives. A spiritual growth study is meant to shake us up, to disturb us, to challenge our understandings, and to push us to new and more wonderful places where God will reveal God's truth.

Each of us has a special way in which we learn best. For some of us, journaling is a helpful way to remember; we write down things that challenge us and questions that we have. For others, it may be notes in the margin or pictures that we draw or poems that we write. Whatever methodology helps you dig deeper in your understanding of the covenants, please use it. This participant's guide will have many different tools that will help you with this study. But the final outcome depends upon you.

The author, Evy McDonald, asks us to take special care in our understanding of the biblical texts. We need to remember that different parts of the Bible were written at different times by different people and were meant to speak to different historical contexts. She suggests that we need to seek to discern the truth of the passages.

The Participant's Guide is organized into four lessons that cover many of the main points of *Living as a Covenant Community*. Each session includes:

- Hearing again the familiar Bible stories that tell of the developing relationship between God and the covenant community.
- Ways to think about how the covenant speaks to realities today, including examples of the work of United Methodist Women.
- Prayers and worship that provide a space to name the opportunities and challenges for Christian discipleship and covenant living before God and our covenant communities.

If you are doing this study with others, you will want to take full advantage of the opportunity to dialogue and struggle together to deepen your understanding of what these covenants mean for you individually and as a wider community.

If you are doing this study on your own, you will want to individualize the group exercises, entering into dialogue with yourself about the questions that you have. Or you may want to correspond with others to share the ideas and questions. Covenant community participation is a collective process. It is very difficult to develop a covenant relationship alone. Community is the implication of covenant. We need God and we need each other.

Consider creating a prayer and worship space while you are doing this study, a place where you can withdraw to in quiet. You might want to include a candle, the Bible, and a small pitcher that you can add water to during each lesson as you learn about a new covenant and add to your insights.

SESSION 1

God as Covenant Maker:
The Covenant of Care and Grace

Preparation

Read the Introduction and Chapters 1 and 2 of *Living as a Covenant Community*, Appendix B, and Genesis 1, 3.

Goals

- To develop an understanding of the meaning of "covenant" from our personal understanding, the Hebrew words, and from traditional and contemporary Jewish community understandings.
- To explore covenant making as God's way of establishing a relationship with humanity through the biblical accounts of God, creation, and Adam and Eve.

Words to Remember

"God created human beings; made them godlike, reflecting God's nature. He created them male and female. God blessed them: "Prosper! Reproduce! Fill the earth! Take charge!" (Genesis 1:27, *The Message*).

Opening Song

Sing one of the following:

"Amen Sikudumisa," *The Faith We Sing*, no. 2067
"Our God is an Awesome God," *The Faith We Sing*, no. 2040

Defining Covenant

Review the section titled "Overview of Covenants" in Chapter 1 of the text as well as the Hebrew terms in the section below it, and then ask the following questions:

- What is your definition of the word "covenant"? Is it about legal agreements or marriage? Does it mean something positive or something negative to you?
- Consider the Hebrew words *berîth* and *hesed* in light of the material in Appendix B, which reads: "The Hebrew word *berîth* traditionally referred to covenant that signified an agreement between two parties. But the word *hesed*, which is used less frequently, gives us the deeper meaning of covenant as the kindness or graciousness of God toward humanity in establishing a relationship."

The First Covenant: God as Covenant Maker and God's Covenant People— the Covenant of Care and Grace

LISTENING TO THE SCRIPTURE, GENESIS 1 AND 3

As you listen to the scripture, put yourself in an attitude of prayer. You may want to use the *Lectio Divina* process as you read and listen to the passages.

It is a prayerful way of Bible study that encourages reading, meditation, prayer, and what is called "rest in the word of God." Read the passages aloud slowly and carefully perhaps two or three times, pausing between each reading.

GENESIS 1:26–28: THE CREATION OF HUMANKIND

Then God said, "Let us make humankind in our image, according to our likeness; and let them have dominion over the fish . . . birds . . . cattle . . . over all the wild animals . . . over every creeping thing that creeps upon the earth" (Genesis 1:26).

God spoke: "Let us make human beings in our image, make them reflecting our nature so they can be responsible for the fish . . . birds . . . cattle, and, yes, Earth itself" (Genesis 1:26, *The Message*).

By God's grace, a relationship is established in which humanity is to be like God, carrying forth God's intention for the world. The text points to the communal nature of God, a recognition of the inner community within God—Creator, Christ, and Holy Spirit. The author further defines this communal nature of God as an egalitarian and harmonious relationship in "The Call to Be a Covenantal Community" in Chapter 1.

- What aspects of God do "in our likeness" or "reflecting God's nature" bring to mind? What is the relationship between God's loving and creative nature and God's intention for the community?
- What demand/responsibility does it place on the covenant community (Adam and Eve) in relationship to the rest of creation? Is that what reflecting God's nature means?

GENESIS 3:1–13

Read the second part of the story relating to the Covenant of Care and Grace in Genesis 3:1–13. The story continues with Adam and Eve's encounter with

the tree of knowledge and the serpent. God established the covenant through the creation process and gave humanity responsibility. Now we see the first action of the covenant community, which reveals something about us all.

Listen to the serpent's conversation with Eve: "God knows that the moment you eat from that tree, you'll see what's really going on. You'll be just like God, knowing everything, ranging all the way from good to evil" (Genesis 3:4–5, *The Message*). Does something about this sound familiar? Consider the following questions:

- What do you think was going through the minds of Adam and Eve (the community), when they were in the midst of this wonderful creation?
- What is the difference between being created, "reflecting God's nature," and the voice of temptation saying, "You'll see what's really going on. You'll be just like God." What does the experience tell us about human nature? Did Adam and Eve create a crisis where there did not have to be one?
- Imagine being a part of that first covenant community: Put yourself in the mind of Adam ("she gave it to me") and Eve ("the serpent seduced me"). Can you develop some additional justifications for their response to the serpent? Why did they choose to eat from the tree of knowledge? Why did they want to be just like God? Does anything like that ever happen to us as a community or as individuals?

WHAT IS THE MEANING OF THE COVENANT FOR OUR LIVES/THE COVENANT COMMUNITY TODAY?

Review the author's story of her personal health crisis in Chapter 1, "How Does This Covenant Inform Our Christian Discipleship?," where she reflects on God's guidance and her own stubbornness in finding her path.

Compare the experience of Adam and Eve to our own faith journeys, the gift of God's caring and moments of crisis and temptation when we want to depend upon ourselves rather than upon the promises of God.

Take time to think alone or with a partner about your own faith journey and its moments of crisis. How did you respond? Was it with your own insights or did you depend upon the insights of faith? Were you tempted to listen to the voices of privilege or greed or selfishness? Write down your responses for yourself or share them with a friend.

Using Appendix A as a starting place, develop a short list that shows examples of faith responses to current crises like climate change, such as the 13 Steps to Sustainability or congregational efforts like Be Just. Be Green.

Develop a second list using Appendix A to identify moments of opportunity for the covenant community that may reflect the difficulty of the task of obedience in the midst of fear and crisis, like a contemporary version of the temptation that is recorded in Genesis 3. Such is the temptation to follow our own knowledge or popular opinion or corporate justifications rather than listening for the guidance of God and resisting what our author calls "God nudges."

PREPARING FOR CLOSING PRAYERS:
WRITING A PSALM FOR TODAY

The writers of the Psalms understood the rhythm of the covenant relationship as one of praise, followed by complaint and worry and ending with praise again.[1]

Using your own experience complete the following prayer modeled from Psalm 40:

(Praise) **I waited patiently for God . . .**
(Praise for the care and the grace of the covenant God in the life of the community. *Name your own examples of blessings, personal and communal.*)
(Complaint) **Troubles surround us . . .**
(*Name the temptations and challenges of the covenant community that you identified.*)

Save us God, come quickly. We are needy and need help.
(*Add a second praise about the joy of the responsibility for the care of creation and the work for social justice.*)

God you are my guide; God you are my God. Please act right away. Help us.

Closing Prayers

Light the covenant candle and add a small amount of water to the covenant pitcher to symbolize the gift of the Covenant of Care and Grace.

Ask participants who are willing to offer their Psalms for today as the closing prayers.

Closing Song

"Our God is an Awesome God," *The Faith We Sing*, no. 2040

Endnotes

1. Walter Brueggemann, *The Covenanted Self: Explorations in Law and Covenant* (Minneapolis: Fortress Press, 1999), 6–8.

 SESSION 2

Covenant-Keeper God and Faithful and Obedient Covenant People: The Covenant of Redemption & Safety and the Covenant of Blessing

Preparation

Read the Introduction and Chapters 2 and 3 in *Living as a Covenant Community*.

Goals

- To learn how God expands the covenant relationship in periods of crisis and fear for the covenant community.
- To consider the importance of great trust and acts of faithfulness by the covenant community.

Words to Remember

"Faith is the assurance of things hoped for, the conviction of things not seen" (Hebrews 11:1).

"God remembered Noah… His remembering is an act of gracious engagement with his covenant partner, an act of committed compassion. It asserts that God is not preoccupied with himself but with his covenant partner, creation."[1]

Opening Song

Sing a favorite song such as one of the hymns listed below:

- "Great Is Thy Faithfulness," *The United Methodist Hymnal*, no. 140 (one verse)
- "My Heavenly Father Watches Over Me," *African American Heritage Hymnal*, no. 144
- "God Will Take Care of You," *The United Methodist Hymnal*, no. 130

Listening to the Biblical Texts: Considering the Experiences of Noah and Abraham

In this session, we will identify the fears and uncertainties of Noah and Abraham and their communities and consider how they overcame the moments of doubt with trust and faithfulness.

Review "Understanding the Story" in Chapter 2 for the context of the story of Noah and the building of the ark.

CONSIDERING THE EXPERIENCES OF NOAH— THE COVENANT OF REDEMPTION AND SAFETY

- **Genesis 6:5–13** The earth was filled with violence and corruption. God vowed to destroy the earth. But Noah found favor with God.
- **Genesis 8:20–22** When the rain stopped, Noah built an altar and made a burnt offering. God vowed to never again destroy the earth.
- **Genesis 9:1–17** The terms of the Covenant of Redemption and Safety are established. The rainbow is a symbol of the covenant.

Review "Understanding the Story" in Chapter 3 for the context of the story of Abraham and Sarah.

CONSIDERING THE EXPERIENCES OF ABRAHAM— THE COVENANT OF BLESSING

- **Genesis 12:1–7** God directs Abram to a new land and promises to make him a great nation.
- **Genesis 15:1–6** God promises Abram offspring and countless descendants even though Sarai is barren. Abram believed God's promise.
- **Genesis 16** Abram and Sarai take matters into their own hands to ensure Abram has descendants.
- **Genesis 17** God's covenant with Abram promises he will be the father of many nations and circumcision is the covenant symbol and requirement for future generations.

After reading the texts, try to imagine what Noah and Abraham may have been thinking during these experiences. You might want to create a monologue or a dialogue that expresses their thoughts, the difficulties of obedience and faithfulness, and their responses to God's covenant blessings. For example: Noah—I know God promised to save me and my family, but I began to think it was never going to stop raining and I didn't know what we were going to do if we never saw land again; after all God promised to destroy the earth. Abraham—The number of family and friends is really quite small, how can we possibly take over a whole land? Is God going to fight against the Canaanites?

THE COVENANT COMMUNITY TODAY: WHAT DOES IT MEAN TO BE A FAITHFUL COVENANT COMMUNITY?

Consider individually or share with a partner your personal crises of faith that may have been similar to the experiences of Noah (the storms of our lives) and Abraham (at the edge of the unknown in our personal and communal lives) where we needed to walk by faith rather than by sight.

Read about the author's experience with her church's decision about a needle exchange program at the beginning of Chapter 3.

In your journal, record personal and community experiences in which members of the covenant community have been challenged to step out into the unknown as they try to be faithful.

You might want to think about this using the covenant symbol of the rainbow:

- Rainbow experiences in which the covenant community has been led by the Spirit to new ways to live out their faith—like the author's experience with the needle exchange program at the beginning of Chapter 3.
- Ways in which the covenant community can be a rainbow or an ark on behalf of justice for others (see Appendix A for examples).

Closing Prayers

Light the covenant candle and add water to the covenant pitcher, symbolizing how each covenant adds to the ones before it.

Use the situations that you have named in today's session as the basis for prayers of thanksgiving to close today. At the end of each thought repeat the response, "God, your servants are listening." The response indicates that the prayer has not ended and affirms the openness of the community to hear God's messages for us; we are learning to be faithful in the best and worst of times.

Endnotes

1. Walter Brueggemann, *Genesis: Interpretation: A Bible Commentary for Teaching and Preaching* (Louisville: John Knox Press, 1982), 85.

# SESSION 3

God the Equipper
and God's Covenant Nation:
The Covenant of Guidance and Law

Preparation

Read the following:

- **Chapter 4:** *Living as a Covenant Community,* "Understanding the Story," "What Does Making the Covenant Say About Moses?," and "Understanding the Covenant, Its Blessings and Conditions"
- **Exodus 19** Moses and the covenant community at Mount Sinai
- **Exodus 20:1–17** The Ten Commandments
- **Deuteronomy 5–6** The Ten Commandments
- **Deuteronomy 10:12–22** Justice for widows and orphans and strangers
- **Leviticus 25:1–7** The Sabbatical Year

Goals

- To increase your understanding of the laws handed down by Moses as a detailed articulation of the elements of the covenant for the community/nation.
- To ponder the relevance of the commandments and laws to our lives today.

Words to Remember

"I am the Lord your God, who brought you out of the land of Egypt, out of the house of slavery; you shall have no other gods before me" (Exodus 20:2–3).

"'You shall love the Lord your God with all your heart, and with all your soul, and with all your mind, and with all your strength.' The second is this, 'You shall love your neighbor as yourself.' There is no other commandment greater than these." Then the scribe said to him, 'You are right, Teacher; you have truly said that 'he is one, and besides him there is no other'" (Mark 12:30–32).

Opening Song

"What Does the Lord Require of You?" *The Faith We Sing*, no. 2174

Considering the Commandments

"Do not think that I have come to abolish the Law or the Prophets; I have come not to abolish but to fulfill" (Matthew 5:17).

McDonald has suggested that the commandments are about three things: defending the oppressed; doing what's right, even if it means criticizing your own people; and remaining faithful wherever you are. The commandments gave structure to the spiritual, social, and political life of the Israelites.

Reflecting the author's discussion in Chapter 4, we will consider the commandments and laws in three parts: loving God, developing a caring community, and the praxis of economic and environmental justice.

PART 1: LOVING GOD: COMMANDMENTS 1–3

Prepare yourself and your space for prayerful reflection on the covenants and laws. If you are alone, slowly speak out loud a commandment three times, pausing for at least one minute of silence between each reading to encourage yourself to deepen your understanding of the commandment. If you are in a group, ask each member to speak aloud the words of the commandments.

- "I am the Lord your God, who brought you out of the land of Egypt, out of the house of slavery; you shall have no other gods before me" (Exodus 20:2–3).
- "You shall love the Lord your God with all your heart, and with all your soul, and with all your might" (Deuteronomy 6:5).
- "You shall not make wrongful use of the name of the Lord your God, for the Lord will not acquit anyone who misuses his name" (Exodus 20:7).

After meditatively reading the commandments, ask yourself the following questions:

- What are some examples of my experience of loving God?
- How well am I doing at loving God?

PART 2: BEING A GOOD NEIGHBOR: COMMANDMENTS 4–10

These commandments cover the topics of work, slavery, and rest (Exodus 20:8–11); honoring parents (Exodus 20:12); murder (Exodus 20:13); adultery (Exodus 20:14); stealing (Exodus 20:15); false witness (Exodus 20:16); and coveting the spouse of a neighbor and the property of others (Exodus 20:17).

Read the text of these commandments slowly and carefully out loud, again pausing to give yourself and your spirit time to listen for their meaning.

After meditatively reading the commandments, ask yourself the following questions:

- What do these commandments mean for the community?
- How could a community, a nation, or a neighborhood see these as collective rules for matters of wages or loans or use of political power rather than rules for personal behavior?

PART 3: THE PRAXIS OF ECONOMIC AND ENVIRONMENTAL JUSTICE FOR A NATION

Next, we will look at God's instruction for the sabbatical year and jubilee year. Following the same pattern, read the text slowly.
Leviticus 25:1–7 The Sabbatical Year
Leviticus 25:8–9 The Jubilee Year

After meditatively reading the commandments, ask yourself:
- How do these laws build economic and environmental justice?

Covenant Living Today

"God called the Israelites, and us today, to not blindly obey, but to listen to God, and let our love for God lead us to do what is right in God's eyes" (Chapter 4, "The Blessings for Keeping the Covenant and Curses (Consequences) for Breaking It").

Read McDonald's account in Chapter 4 of *Living as a Covenant Community* about her encounter with two boys at Best Buy. Hear her regret at her failure to respond to their moment of need and her lost opportunity to be a blessing to them.

Take a few moments to think about contemporary examples of the work of the covenant community in individual and collective crises through the lens of the Ten Commandments. Use the examples in Appendix A to start your thinking.

Closing Prayers

Use the insights from your prayerful consideration of the covenants and laws to complete the prayer below, adapted from Psalm 106.

Praise the Lord! Give thanks to God for God is good; still, God heard the troubles we were in—the destruction of the planet, and the persistence of racism, the growth of economic injustice and _____, heard our cries even when we were feeling exiled from God's purpose.

God showed us how to_____ because _____.

Thanks be to God, the Covenant Equipper, who showed us how to strive to be a faithful and just community.

Closing Song

"What Does the Lord Require of You?" *The Faith We Sing*, no. 2174

 SESSION 4

Covenant-Fulfilling God and Grace-Filled Covenant Community: The Covenants of Eternal Rule, Everlasting Friendship, and the Everlasting Covenant

Preparation

Read the following:

- **2 Samuel 7:1–17** God's covenant promises
- **1 Chronicles 17** God's covenant with David
- **Psalm 89:3–4** God's covenant with David
- **1 Samuel 18–20** Jonathan's covenant of friendship with David
- **Jeremiah 31** Foretelling of the return from exile and the new covenant
- **Acts 10:34–43** Good news is for all people
- **Philippians 2:1–5** Disciplines for the covenant community
- **Chapters 5 and 6** in *Living as a Covenant Community*

Goals

- To understand God's Covenant of Eternal Rule with David as an elaboration of the covenant promises to Abraham and Moses for the development of the nation and its implications for modern church structures.

- To review the Covenant of Everlasting Friendship between David and Jonathan as a model for human relationships and a foretaste of the sacrifice of Jesus.
- To consider how the ministry and life of Jesus represent the fullest articulation of God's relationship with the covenant community/humanity in the Everlasting Covenant.

Words to Remember

"The days are surely coming, says the Lord, when I will make a new covenant with the house of Israel and the house of Judah . . . this is the covenant that I will make with the house of Israel . . . says the Lord: I will put my law within them, and I will write it on their hearts; and I will be their God, and they shall be my people" (Jeremiah 31:31, 33).

" . . . be of the same mind, having the same love, being in full accord and of one mind. Do nothing from selfish ambition or conceit, but in humility regard others as better than yourselves. Let each of you look not to your own interests, but to the interests of others. Let the same mind be in you that was in Christ Jesus" (Philippians 2:2–5).

Opening Song

Sing one of the following from The Faith We Sing:

- "Lord I Lift Your Name on High," no. 2088
- "Siyahamba," no. 2235

Considering the Covenant of Eternal Rule—God's Covenant with David

Review 2 Samuel 7 and *Living as a Covenant Community*, Chapter 5, "Understanding the Story."

In 2 Samuel 7:1–17 we learn of the four elements of the covenant between God and David: everlasting reign, rest from his enemies, a home to live in, and the land for his people. But David wanted to build a temple to house the ark of the covenant (2 Samuel 7:18–29), which for many years had been a movable worship place, as a sign of his gratitude to God. However, God told David that this temple would only be built by his son.

Let's consider for a moment David's failure to meet his personal goal and build the temple in light of our own experiences. How important are the buildings and structures of the church?

- Might David have had what the author described as "the dark night of the soul"—a sense of frustration at not being able to complete the temple himself? Have you ever felt that way?
- "As a people, the church is really not a place to which we go but the dynamic community that actively reaches out in Christ's love to the needy and underprivileged of our society" (Chapter 5). What, from your own experiences might reflect the truth of this statement?

Considering David's Covenant of Everlasting Friendship with Jonathan

Review 1 Samuel 18–20 and *Living as a Covenant Community*, Chapter 5, "Understanding the Covenant Between Jonathan and David" and "The Covenant of Everlasting Friendship."

The covenant between David and Jonathan represents an important picture of ideal human relationships. The sacrifices they needed to make often involved deep understanding of the love of neighbor, especially with its relationship to injustice and issues of power. The covenant also can inform our relationship with God and Jesus as well as with our neighbor. "A sacred covenant relationship meant you did not make decisions without taking into

account how your actions or choices would affect your covenant partner"
(Chapter 5, "The Elements of the Covenant"). From the relationship
between David and Jonathan, we learn that a covenant can transcend
cultural and family loyalties, encouraging us to embrace the stranger and
the alien.

- What can we learn from the elements that symbolized the friendship
  between David and Jonathan—the exchange of armor, the exchange of
  names, and the willingness to sacrifice?
- Can you think about a time when you have been asked to enter into
  such a radical friendship?

Considering Jesus
and the Everlasting Covenant

To understand the context for the coming of Jesus as the Everlasting
Covenant, it is important to first read Jeremiah 31:31–34. The Jeremiah
text was written in the context of the Israelite exile with the promise that
a new covenant will be given. Take some time to think about the historical
context into which Jesus was born—a period of colonialism and a period
of crisis marked by conflicting political and religious values. Does this
seem like ripe conditions for another development of God's covenantal
relationship with the covenant community?

WHAT DOES JESUS HAVE TO DO
WITH THE COVENANT?

It's helpful to recall the elements of the covenants that we have learned about
in this study so far: care, grace, redemption, safety, blessing, guidance, and
eternal rule. We can make a list about each characteristic and then recall from
our knowledge of the ministry of Jesus those occasions when each of these
characteristics of the covenant were integral to his ministry:

- Care—e.g., the healing of the blind man
- Grace—e.g., the promise of grace in the gift of the Holy Spirit
- Redemption—e.g., woman possessed by demons
- Safety—e.g., calming the storm
- Blessing—e.g., creating a new social order that overturns the oppression of the money changers in the Temple
- Guidance—e.g., Beatitudes
- Eternal rule—e.g., a new understanding of power in relationships: the tax collector and the rich, young ruler

Once the lists are made, they can be used to proclaim as a group or individually the covenant-fulfilling activity of Jesus by recalling each of the activities beginning with the phrase "I am a witness to the goodness of God . . . " For example: "I am a witness to the goodness of God as we experienced the revitalization of our church when we thought we would have to close the doors."

The Meaning of the Covenant Today: Exploring the Power of Living in the Covenant

In his book *The Covenanted Self*, Theologian and Old Testament scholar Walter Brueggemann has suggested that "we are bound to a God for whom the neighbor comes first."[1] Brueggemann's interpretation of the apostle Paul's letter to the Philippians is that Paul believed that the church was not to conduct business or settle disputes in the same way as other communities. Different disciplines and ways of being in relationship must be practiced because of the covenantal relationship between the community and God.

It is important that we attempt to affirm for ourselves what it means for our way of living to be a covenant community that is bound to a God for whom the neighbor comes first (Chapter 6). In Philippians 2:1 Paul recommends using the following disciplines:

- Encouragement in Christ
- Consolation from love
- Sharing in the Spirit
- Compassion
- Sympathy

Using Appendix A as a starting point, review and name concrete examples of action by the covenant community that demonstrate each of these disciplines.

A yardstick for measuring the actions of the covenant community might be Philippians 2:3–4:

"Do nothing from selfish ambition or conceit, but in humility regard others as better than yourselves. Let each of you look not to your own interests, but to the interests of others."

One final question we need to ask ourselves is if we practice all of these disciplines found in Philippians 2, could we say to ourselves that we understand what it means to, "Let the same mind be in you that was in Christ Jesus?"

Time for Commitment

The end of our spiritual growth study on the covenants is an opportunity to use all that we have learned to declare for ourselves our personal commitments to covenant community. We need to ask ourselves what specifically we will do (and how often) as a result of this study. We can name our commitments in four areas:

- **Prayer:** Conversation—even debate—with God to deepen our relationship with our creator and covenant maker. Consider how often and how long you will commit to pray.
- **Advocacy:** Action on behalf of God's just kin-dom. Consider how and where you are called to serve.

- **Intentional growth:** Seeking ways to grow spiritually, emotionally, and mentally and using weekly disciplines to foster that growth as individuals and in community. Consider what disciplines you will use and how often you will employ them.
- **Community life:** Learning how we are to live in community and take seriously the commandments and laws in our life together. Consider who you need to reach out to and how you can deepen your community life.

If you are doing this study in a group, you will have the opportunity for each person to share their commitment. If you are doing this study individually, you might want to record your commitments and post them somewhere in your home in order to keep track of your progress. You will also want to share your commitments with others in your covenant community. Covenant is a community process.

Closing Worship

Light the covenant candle and add water to the covenant pitcher, leaving room at the top, affirming God's ongoing revelation to the covenant community and affirming our commitments to covenant community.

If you are in a group allow each person to take the opportunity if they wish to share their covenant commitments with the group.

CLOSING LITANY:
WESLEY'S COVENANT PRAYER (ADAPTED)

Read in unison.

> We are no longer our own, but yours.
> Put us to what you will,

Place us with whom you will.

Put us to doing, put us to suffering.

Let us be put to work for you or set aside for you,

Praised for you or criticized for you.

Let us be full, let us be empty.

Let us have all things, let us have nothing.

We freely and fully surrender all things to your glory and sacrifice.

And now, a wonderful and holy God, COVENANT MAKER, COVENANT KEEPER, AND COVENANT EQUIPPER, you are ours, and we are yours.

So be it. And the covenant, which we have made on earth, let it also be made in heaven. Amen.

Closing Song

"The Summons," *The Faith We Sing,* no. 2130

Benediction (unison)

"Now to [God] who by the power at work within us is able to accomplish abundantly far more than all we can ask or imagine, to [God] be glory in the church and in Christ Jesus to all generations, forever and ever. Amen" (Ephesians 3:20–21).

APPENDIX A

United Methodist Women as a Covenant Community

Session 1: Faith Responses and Moments of Opportunity

ENVIRONMENTAL JUSTICE

- Five United Methodist Women members have been trained to act as jurisdictional guides to implement the 13 Steps to Sustainability in the life of conferences and communities.
- The jurisdictional guide in the Rocky Mountain Conference is studying and working to address toxic flooding of the southern Ute tribe.
- A Be Just. Be Green. team in the Holston Conference has started intentional sharing and working to implement the 13 Steps to Sustainability across the annual conference.
- United Methodist Women has partnered with young women (21–38 years old) and formed the New Generation Climate Justice Group. They began a five-month home study of climate change issues in order to begin working more intentionally on these issues with the support of their local communities.
- The United Methodist Women Be Just. Be Green. initiative encourages United Methodist Women members to actively resist prevailing popular and public opinion and corporate power justifications, and challenge our own economic and social power in order to listen to the voice of God, using intentional decisions and lifestyle changes to begin the movement towards a new way of life.

RACIAL JUSTICE/ENVIRONMENTAL JUSTICE

- United Methodist Women actively engaged in advocacy efforts in regards to the crisis in Flint, Michigan. The organization and its members called out injustices such as popular calls for tax breaks, particularly for the wealthy, which meant austerity programs for everyone else; state government authority for emergency management strategies that neglected and silenced the voice of the people; higher utility rates to cover the problems created by corporate polluters; and structural racism that perpetuates injustices as seen in underfunded schools, lack of public transportation, high rates of maternal and child mortality, and now lead poisoning.

MATERNAL AND CHILD HEALTH

- Community Development for All People, a National Mission Institution in Columbus, Ohio, is working to honor the creation of new life and address issues of infant mortality by hosting a "first birthday party" to engage women who are pregnant or mothers of infants with the goal of connecting them to resources and support that will hopefully reduce infant deaths.
- Neighborhood Services Organization, a National Mission Institution in Oklahoma City runs a WIC center that coaches pregnant and new mother s on nursing, pregnancy, nutrition, etc. It is strategically located next door to a private market that has WIC-approved foods.

Session 2: Stepping Out in Faith: Covenant Community as a Rainbow or Ark for Justice

MATERNAL AND CHILD HEALTH

- National Seminar participants aware of racial disparities in birth outcomes joined in a protest to save the neonatal intensive care unit at one of Chicago's hospitals that serves the underserved. Local units also joined the coalition for ongoing work to save the hospital's pediatric unit.
- Young women from the New York Limitless group participated in a Days for Girls advocacy training sponsored by United Methodist Women during the 2016 United Nations Commission on the Status of Women. As a result they began raising money for Days for Girls reusable hygiene kits.

ECONOMIC JUSTICE

- New York Annual Conference President joined the Coalition of Immokalee Workers calling for the fast food chain Wendy's to sign a fair food agreement to support a wage increase by paying an additional penny per pound for the tomatoes it purchases and require a human rights–based code of conduct to be implemented on the farms that grow their tomatoes.
- Several United Methodist Women leaders, inspired by the 2015 National Seminar, are now leading a workshop with United for a Fair Economy titled "Overworked and Undervalued: Women, Race and the Economy" to spur more United Methodist Women members into action.
- A local United Methodist Women leader in the Northern Illinois Conference has been active in efforts to increase the minimum wage to $15 per hour, including a focus on the fast food industry.

- Gordon Memorial United Methodist Church in Nashville partnered with the Children's Defense Fund Freedom School® Program. Freedom Schools® are free summer programs that focus on reading and provide other summer experiences for low-income and at-risk children. The six-week program also has a strong focus on advocacy, encouraging parents to work for change in their public schools and communities.

- United Methodist Women called for justice in communities and re-committed itself to continuing work to end systemic racism. The call for action included expanding conversations on racial justice by using the Showing up for Racial Justice Police Brutality Action Kit; regularly reexamining United Methodist Women obligations under the Charter for Racial Justice; viewing media through a social justice and racial justice lens; and using the Reading Program and annual studies to deepen understanding of other people's experience of injustice.

Session 3: The Work of the Covenant Community in Individual and Collective Crises

ECONOMIC JUSTICE

You shall not steal.

- El Pueblo Immigration Services, a mission of the Seashore District in Mississippi, received a Call to Prayer and Self-Denial Grant in 2014 from United Methodist Women to help unbanked and underserved Hispanic immigrants handle their financial affairs and consumer needs, protecting themselves from fees, predatory lending practices, and high interest rates through a financial literacy program.

Observe the Sabbath day and keep it holy . . . Remember that you were slaves in Egypt and the Lord your God brought you out . . . With a mighty hand.

- United Methodist Women is encouraging members to tell Congress it's time for a moral and just minimum wage and advocate for increasing the minimum wage in their community or state to $15 per hour.
- United Methodist Women members are encouraged to join Arise Chicago, an advocacy and education partnership between faith communities and workers, and learn how faith groups are engaged in supporting workers and fighting wage theft.

RACIAL JUSTICE

You shall not murder.

- United Methodists are joining other faith groups in the national religious campaign against torture. The campaign seeks to make torture visible and also to ban its use by signing the National Religious Campaign against Solitary Confinement statement and joining state and local campaigns.
- United Methodist Women from the Great Plains and Rio Texas conferences have been active in local campaigns to end the death penalty. In Nebraska, a United Methodist Women leader participated in a vigil to try and stop the governor from reinstating the death penalty.

Neither shall you desire your neighbor's house, or field, or male or female slave, or ox, or donkey, or anything that belongs to your neighbor.

- Following the 2008 General Conference Resolution, "Healing Relationships with Indigenous Persons," United Methodist Women of the Yellowstone Conference pioneered reconciliation efforts with the Northern Cheyenne tribe in light of the 1864 participation of Methodist minister Col. John Chivington in the attack on the unarmed encampment at Sand Creek.

- Across the United States, twenty United Methodist annual conferences are engaging in healing relationships with indigenous people groups, including work in Oklahoma and in Alabama.

MATERNAL AND CHILD HEALTH

Honor your father and your mother.

- Three women die each day in the United States from childbirth, disproportionally affecting women of color, low-income, and rural families—this is the highest maternal mortality rate among industrialized nations. United Methodist Women is advocating for Maternal Death Review Panels in the nineteen states that do not have them.
- In many parts of the world, women are reluctant to seek care because of negative experiences. In this quadrennium, United Methodist Women will be joining an international movement advocating for respectful maternity care to eliminate disrespect and abuse and encourage women to receive the care they need before, during, and after giving birth.

Session 4: Covenant Community Actions

ECONOMIC JUSTICE

- United Methodist Women members are encouraged to read *The Age of Dignity: Preparing for the Elder Boom in a Changing America.* Also consider making a pledge to commit to fair workplace standards and joining the Hand-To-Hand Network of Caring across America.
- United Methodist Women members are encouraged to read *Forked!*, a book about women restaurant workers. They can also download the Diner's Guide to Ethical Eating app to help determine which

restaurants they should frequent. The app highlights restaurants that pay workers fair wages and benefits, and allow patrons to rate them on racially equality through Yelp!.

RACIAL JUSTICE/ENVIRONMENTAL JUSTICE

- United Methodist Women members are urged to join the Color of Change campaign to restore funding to the Center for Disease Control's Healthy Homes/Lead Poisoning Prevention Program for fiscal year 2017.
- United Methodist Women members are urged to look at safe drinking water issues in their own community and how they may disproportionately impact communities of color and call for state and federal accountability for communities facing toxic drinking water.

ECONOMIC JUSTICE/RACIAL JUSTICE

- In response to the unfair practices of family detention centers and United Methodist Women's Campaign to End Family Detention, 250 Texan United Methodist Women members went to Dilly, Texas, in May 2015 to join a protest outside of the family detention center there to call for an end to family detentions.

MATERNAL HEALTH/GENDER JUSTICE

- The Neighborhood Center in Harrisburg, Pennsylvania, is a United Methodist Women–supported National Mission Institution with programs for children and support activities for young mothers. The summertime free and reduced-price lunch program is staffed by United Methodist Women members from the Susquehanna Conference.

- A grant from United Methodist Women in 2011 to the Nyadire United Methodist hospital in Zimbabwe helped fund the establishment of the School of Midwifery, where one hundred midwives graduate each year with emergency training in obstetric and newborn care.
- United Methodist Women members in Huntington, West Virginia, are assisting with HER Place, an educational center founded in 2013 by a United Methodist Women member. It serves drug-addicted women and their children in the community through educational and support programs as well as other services.

ENVIRONMENTAL JUSTICE/GENDER JUSTICE

- A United Methodist Women Call to Prayer and Self-Denial Grant has enabled women's groups in rural Uganda to purchase seeds and tools and learn new methods to improve women's status in their communities.

APPENDIX B

Conversation Between Maharat Rori Picker Neiss and Kathleen Stone

This is an excerpt of a conversation between Maharat Rori Picker Neiss, executive director of the Jewish Community Relations Council of St. Louis, Missouri, and Kathleen Stone, former United Methodist Women executive and current pastor at Wharton United Community Church at St. John in Wharton, New Jersey.

On the Meaning of the Covenant

On the most basic level we see it as being the relationship, a relationship that involves a requirement from both parties. . . . But the crucial difference when we start talking about a religious covenant, we recognize it as something of an absurd statement to say that we can be in covenant with God to the extent that there is no way that there can be equity in this covenant. . . . So within the covenant there is a sudden sense of generosity. The covenant is not some kind of business deal. It is really an act of graciousness on the part of God in the exchange.

The Meaning of *Berîth* and *Hesed*

Berîth is the word that we often use when we are talking about covenants. In the Torah, we talk about Abraham, we talk about *berîth*—the covenant between parties. And that we understand as a kind of business deal. We talk about the ritual of circumcision, we talk about *berîth*. . . . *hesed* we would not typically use in relationship to covenant. *Hesed* we really understand meaning kindness . . . (covenant). Yes, this is a kindness of God. This is God's *hesed*, God's kindness. *Hesed* is really unidirectional.

About the Covenant Relationship

God creates the world and the relationship starts to evolve as people are given autonomy. . . . And so the relationship between us has to change. That's one way to look at God's promises to Adam and Eve, but what God promises to Noah is going to be different after sin has overtaken the world. . . . We don't see covenants replacing the prior ones, but the covenant that begins with Abraham and then with Moses is very much a particular covenant whereas the covenant with Adam and Noah are universal.

The Jewish Covenant Community

God has a covenant with humanity, but God also has a unique role for the Jewish people in the world. That unique role doesn't replace the relationship of others. But we very much see ourselves as having a responsibility in the world. . . . It's really not my real concern to figure out your role but it is my concern to try to figure out my role. And I need to be focused on what it is I have responsibility for in this world.

It seems like God is saying: I'm going to give you all these things and in exchange I want you to walk my path. . . . But a very crucial part of the Jewish faith, when we don't follow the path, God is able to rescind some of the gifts but never break the covenant. So we get kicked out of the land of Israel but we never lose the covenant with God.

The Covenant and Daily Life

It worked its way into my life in the everyday ritual. The way I choose to honor the Sabbath, and the holidays. All of those are going to be reflected in this relationship that I feel that I have. . . . . But I very much believe that all those rituals are meant to push us to think about what they mean in the broader world. That's where we have a responsibility as Jews to be asking questions about things like Syrian refugees, climate change, hunger, poverty. . . . When I choose to eat matzos on Sabbath. . . . I need to ask myself what that means that we were slaves in Egypt. That freedom doesn't exist everywhere in the world. That is something that is a personal question for me. To me the law is love. Love towards God; it is love towards others.

Land

A big part of the promise of the covenant, especially with Abraham, is not only the land, but becoming a people. And so what does it mean to become a people? So people seem to be tied to land. . . . In the modern context: what does it mean to be a people and what does it mean to be a people without a land? Where is our identity? So some will say for the context of the time that in that context of becoming a people was the promise of growing as a people and then having a land. And that's what made them a people.

The Special Responsibility and the Covenant

There is another challenge to the covenant equation, which is that historically for the Jewish community it has come to mean a covenant of suffering.

Somehow what it meant to be chosen as Jewish people meant to be persecuted throughout history. . . . Because you're trying to reconcile what is my special role that I am given with the land and what is my responsibility to protect myself when historically every culture seems to want to exterminate the Jewish people?

Brueggemann's Interpretation of Canaan

Typically, we talk about Canaan as a literal place, what became the precursor to the land of Israel. So, it's interesting to understand because we do understand the Canaanites as not being a righteous people. . . . And so it becomes one way for us to justify what has transpired. It also becomes a beautiful way of universalizing some of the message. So, it is not about conquering this one land but about combating exploitation in all lands. I don't think that goes against Jewish thought but it is not traditionally how we have understood it. We have understood it in a very literal sense.

Israel

It's one of my favorite topics how in the second [exile] the rabbis kept Judaism alive when it should have died out, given that so many of our rituals were about the holy Temple and Jerusalem. And so it's fascinating the way in which that happens and so within that talking about Israel within the prayers was about talking about some sort of lofty goal. And not necessarily in a literal land. . . . But, when we talk about Israel we talk about restoration of the Temple, of the kingdom, of the peoplehood that we had. . . . And so, when it started to become a possibility in the land of Israel . . . many Jews felt . . . that only God could bring the people back. It was really only after 1967 after this Six-Day War . . . that we start to see a shift into what we call religious Zionism. Yes, [God] goes back to the covenant. Yes, the idea that God gave us this land and then kicked us out of this land. But it was always meant to be our land. Now we're seeing a budding up of this religious worldview with the political movement. . . . Everything in our prayers talked about this ideal futuristic perception and then all of a sudden we have the United Nations saying sure there can be a country called Israel.

Maharat Rori Picker Neiss is executive director of the Jewish Community Relations Council of St. Louis, Missori. Maharat *is the title given to Orthodox Jewish women who are trained in the Torah and spiritual leadership.*

🔖 About the Author

elmira Nazombe has worked in the areas of social and economic justice and human rights for over five decades. She was an executive secretary for racial justice for United Methodist Women for seven years. She has worked for a variety of ecumenical organizations including Church World Service, All Africa Conference of Churches, and National Christian Council of Kenya. She has been active for the last twenty years as a social justice educator. She is the author of the mission study *Globalization and Its Impact on People's Lives*; co-author of the leader's guide for the mission study *God's People in an Urban Culture*. She was part of the team of writers for *A Mission Journey: A Handbook for Volunteers*. She is trained as both an educator and an urban planner. She holds a doctorate in education, focused on using education to work for social and economic transformation. She currently teaches social justice courses at Rutgers University in New Jersey, hoping to nurture a new generation of social justice activists.